Ninja Woodfire Ou Electric Grill & Smoker Cookbook

1300 Days of Affordable, Easy and Savory Ninja Wood Fire Electric Pellet Smoker Recipes

Andrea R. McAleer

Warning-Disclaimer:

The purpose of this book is to educate and entertain. The author or publisher does not guarantee that anyone following the techniques, suggestions, tips, ideas, or strategies will become successful. The author and publisher shall have neither liability or responsibility to anyone with respect to any loss or damage caused, or alleged to be caused, directly or indirectly by the information contained in this book.

CONTENTS

MEASUREMENT CONVERSIONS 9

Breakfastst Recipes 11

Western Omelet 11

Grilled Sausage Mix 11

Tomato-corn Frittata With Avocado Dressing 12

Bacon And Egg Stuffed Peppers 12

Stuffed Bell Peppers With Italian Maple-glazed Sausage 13

Crustless Broccoli Quiche 13

Bacon And Broccoli Bread Pudding 14

Pesto Egg Croissantwiches 14

Breakfast Tater Tot Casserole 15

Blueberry Dump Cake 15

Grilled Kielbasa And Pineapple Kebabs 16

Breakfast Chilaquiles 16

Asparagus And Cheese Strata 17

Everything Bagel Breakfast Bake 17

Egg And Avocado Burrito 18

Fried Potatoes With Peppers And Onions 18

Banana Chips With Peanut Butter 19

Egg And Sausage Stuffed Breakfast Pockets 19

Spinach Omelet 20

Olives, Kale, And Pecorino Baked Eggs 20

Cornflakes Toast Sticks 21

Avocado Eggs 21

Mushroom And Squash Toast 22

Supersized Family Pizza Omelet 22

Egg And Bacon Nests 23

Apple And Walnut Muffins 23

Nut And Seed Muffins 24

Meats Recipes 25

Potato And Prosciutto Salad 25

Fast Lamb Satay 25

Steak And Lettuce Salad 26

Cheesy Beef Meatballs 26

Crusted Pork Chops With Honey-maple Jalapeño Glaze 27

Smoky Paprika Pork And Vegetable Kabobs 27

Herb And Pesto Stuffed Pork Loin 28

Pepperoni And Bell Pepper Pockets 28

Balsamic Honey Mustard Lamb Chops 29

Brown-sugared Ham 29

Spicy Pork With Candy Onions 30

Italian Sausage And Peppers 30

Rib Eye Steak With Rosemary Butter 31

Spicy Pork Chops With Carrots And Mushrooms 31

Spicy Beef Lettuce Wraps 32

Char Siew 32

Green Curry Beef 33

Homemade Teriyaki Pork Ribs 33

Burnt Ends 34

Crispy Pork Belly Bites 34

Sausage Ratatouille 35

Citrus Carnitas 35

Asian-flavored Steak Kebabs 36

Ranch And Cheddar Pork Chops 36

Beef And Scallion Rolls 37

Tonkatsu 37

Garlic Herb Crusted Lamb 38

Spaghetti Squash Lasagna 38

Stuffed-onion Burgers 39

Korean-style Steak Tips 39

Pork Sausage With Cauliflower Mash 40

Meatless Recipes **40**

Cinnamon-spiced Acorn Squash 40

Flatbread Pizza 41

Crusted Brussels Sprouts With Sage 41

Charred Green Beans With Sesame Seeds 42

Cheese And Spinach Stuffed Portobellos 42

Vegetable And Cheese Stuffed Tomatoes 43

Green Beans With Sun-dried Tomatoes And Feta 43

Arugula And Broccoli Salad 44

Potatoes With Zucchinis 44

Grilled Artichokes With Garlic Aioli 45

Zucchini And Onions Au Gratin 46

Sriracha Golden Cauliflower 46

Chermoula Beet Roast 47

Loaded Zucchini Boats 47

Simple Ratatouille 48

Black Bean And Tomato Chili 48

Asian-inspired Broccoli 49

Double "egg" Plant (eggplant Omelets) 49

Veggie Taco Pie 50

Perfect Grilled Asparagus 50

Tofu, Carrot And Cauliflower Rice 51

Balsamic Mushroom Sliders With Pesto 51

Summer Squash And Zucchini Salad 52

Cheesy Macaroni Balls 52

Bean And Corn Stuffed Peppers 53

Grilled Vegetable Quesadillas 53

Sweet And Spicy Corn On The Cob 54

Mozzarella Broccoli Calzones 54

Grilled Vegetable Pizza 55

Kidney Beans Oatmeal In Peppers 56

Poultry Recipes **56**

Blackened Chicken Breasts 56

Crispy Chicken Strips 57

Lemon And Rosemary Chicken 57

Honey Rosemary Chicken 58

Lime Chicken With Cilantro 58

Garlic Brown-butter Chicken With Tomatoes 59

Nutty Chicken Tenders 59

Blackened Chicken 60

Roasted Cajun Turkey 60

Turkey Stuffed Bell Peppers 61

Mayonnaise-mustard Chicken 61

Spicy Chicken Kebabs 62

Strawberry-glazed Turkey 62

Stuffed Spinach Chicken Breast 63

Spicy Bbq Chicken Drumsticks 63

Adobo Chicken 64

Mini Turkey Meatloaves With Carrot 64

Sweet Chili Turkey Kebabs 65

Grilled Cornish Hens 65

Potato Cheese Crusted Chicken 66

Roasted Chicken Tenders With Veggies 66

Crispy Dill Pickle Chicken Wings 67

Rosemary Turkey Scotch Eggs 67

Herbed Grilled Chicken Thighs 68

Fried Buffalo Chicken Taquitos 68

Buttermilk Ranch Chicken Tenders 69

Simple Whole Chicken Bake 69

Orange And Honey Glazed Duck With Apples 70

Spiced Turkey Tenderloin 70

Chicken Cordon Bleu Roll-ups 71

Sauces, Dips, And Dressings Recipes 72

Lemon Dijon Vinaigrette 72

Cashew Pesto 72

Sides, Snacks & Appetizers Recipes 73

Garlic Fries 73

Mozzarella Sticks 73

Blt With Grilled Heirloom Tomato 74

Cayenne Sesame Nut Mix 74

Dill Pickles 75

Roasted Mixed Nuts 75

Homemade Bbq Chicken Pizza 76

Cheesy Apple Roll-ups 76

Bacon-wrapped Onion Rings And Spicy Aioli 77

Cheesy Crab Toasts 77

Easy Muffuletta Sliders With Olives 78

Rosemary Baked Cashews 78

One-pot Nachos 79

Candied Brussels Sprouts With Bacon 79

Breaded Green Olives 80

Cuban Sandwiches 80

Caramelized Peaches 81

Bruschetta With Tomato And Basil 81

Grilled Carrots With Honey Glazed 82

Cheesy Steak Fries 82

Avocado Egg Rolls 83

Balsamic Broccoli 83

Deluxe Cheese Sandwiches 84

Seafood Recipes **84**

Mom's Lemon-pepper Salmon 84

Buttered Lobster Tails 85

Crusted Codfish 85

Shrimp Boil 86

Tilapia With Cilantro And Ginger 86

Coconut Shrimp With Orange Chili Sauce 87

Tomato-stuffed Grilled Sole 87

Garlic Butter Shrimp Kebabs 88

Honey-walnut Shrimp 88

Desserts Recipes **89**

Apple Pie Crumble 89

Peanut Butter-chocolate Bread Pudding 89

Banana And Walnut Cake 90

Grilled Apple Fries With Caramel Cream Cheese Dip 90

Curry Peaches, Pears, And Plums 91

Mixed Berry And Cream Cheese Puff Pastries 91

Orange Cake 92

Rum Grilled Pineapple Sundaes 92

Coffee Chocolate Cake 93

Chocolate S'mores 93

Orange Coconut Cake 94

Grilled Banana S'mores 94

Grilled Strawberry Pound Cake 95

Blackberry Chocolate Cake 95

Chocolate Molten Cake 96

Oatmeal And Carrot Cookie Cups 96

Lemony Blackberry Crisp 97

Orange And Anise Cake 97

Vanilla Scones 98

Peaches-and-cake Skewers 98

Graham Cracker Cheesecake 99

Ultimate Coconut Chocolate Cake 99

Pound Cake With Mixed Berries 100

Black And White Brownies 100

Pecan Pie 101

Fudge Pie 101

Classic Pound Cake 102

Pumpkin Pudding 102

Simple Corn Biscuits 103

Biscuit Raisin Bread 103

Strawberry Pizza 104

RECIPES INDEX **105**

MEASUREMENT CONVERSIONS

BASIC KITCHEN CONVERSIONS & EQUIVALENTS

DRY MEASUREMENTS CONVERSION CHART

3 TEASPOONS = 1 TABLESPOON = 1/16 CUP

6 TEASPOONS = 2 TABLESPOONS = 1/8 CUP

12 TEASPOONS = 4 TABLESPOONS = 1/4 CUP

24 TEASPOONS = 8 TABLESPOONS = 1/2 CUP

36 TEASPOONS = 12 TABLESPOONS = 3/4 CUP

48 TEASPOONS = 16 TABLESPOONS = 1 CUP

METRIC TO US COOKING CONVER-SIONS

OVEN TEMPERATURES

120 °C = 250 °F

160 °C = 320 °F

180 °C = 350 °F

205 °C = 400 °F

220 °C = 425 °F

LIQUID MEASUREMENTS CONVERSION CHART

8 FLUID OUNCES = 1 CUP = 1/2 PINT = 1/4 QUART

16 FLUID OUNCES = 2 CUPS = 1 PINT = 1/2 QUART

32 FLUID OUNCES = 4 CUPS = 2 PINTS = 1 QUART 1/4 GALLON

128 FLUID OUNCES = 16 CUPS = 8 PINTS = 4 QUARTS = 1 GALLON

BAKING IN GRAMS

1 CUP FLOUR = 140 GRAMS

1 CUP SUGAR = 150 GRAMS

1 CUP POWDERED SUGAR=160 GRAMS

1 CUP HEAVY CREAM = 235 GRAMS

VOLUME

1 MILLILITER=1/5 TEASPOON

5 ML = 1 TEASPOON

15 ML = 1 TABLESPOON

240 ML = 1 CUP OR 8 FLUID OUNCES

1 LITER=34 FL. OUNCES

WEIGHT

1 GRAM = 035 OUNCES

100 GRAMS=3.5 OUNCES

500 GRAMS = 1.1 POUNDS

1 KILOGRAM=35 OUNCES

US TO METRIC COOKING CONVERSIONS

1/5 TSP = 1 ML
1 TSP=5 ML
1 TBSP = 15 ML
1 FL OUNCE = 30 ML
1 CUP=237 ML
1 PINT (2 CUPS) = 473 ML
1 QUART (4 CUPS)=.95 LITER
1GALLON (16 CUPS)=3.8LITERS
1 0Z=28 GRAMS
1 POUND = 454 GRAMS

BUTTER

1 CUP BUTTER=2 STICKS = 8 OUNCES = 230 GRAMS=8 TABLESPOONS

WHAT DOES 1 CUP EQUAL

1 CUP = 8 FLUID OUNCES
1 CUP = 16 TABLESPOONS
1 CUP = 48 TEASPOONS
1 CUP = 1/2 PINT
1 CUP = 1/4 QUART
1 CUP = 1/16 GALLON
1 CUP = 240 ML

BAKING PAN CONVERSIONS

1 CUP ALL-PURPOSE FLOUR=4.5 OZ
1 CUP ROLLED OATS = 3 OZ 1 LARGE EGG = 1.7 OZ
1 CUP BUTTER=80Z 1 CUP MILK = 8 OZ
1 CUP HEAVY CREAM = 8.4 OZ
1 CUP GRANULATED SUGAR=7.1 OZ
1 CUP PACKED BROWN SUGAR = 7.75 OZ
1 CUP VEGETABLE OIL = 7.7 OZ
1 CUP UNSIFTED POWDERED SUGAR = 4.4 OZ

BAKING PAN CONVERSIONS

9-INCH ROUND CAKE PAN= 12 CUPS

10-INCH TUBE PAN =16 CUPS

11-INCH BUNDT PAN = 12 CUPS

9-INCH SPRINGFORM PAN = 10 CUPS

9 X 5 INCH LOAF PAN=8 CUPS

9-INCH SQUARE PAN=8 CUPS

Breakfastst Recipes

Western Omelet

Servings: 2
Cooking Time: 18 To 21 Minutes
Ingredients:
- ¼ cup chopped bell pepper, green or red
- ¼ cup chopped onion
- ¼ cup diced ham
- 1 teaspoon butter
- 4 large eggs
- 2 tablespoons milk
- ⅛ teaspoon salt
- ¾ cup shredded sharp Cheddar cheese

Directions:
1. Select AIR CRISP, set the temperature to 390°F, and set the time to 6 minutes. Select START/STOP to begin preheating.
2. Put the bell pepper, onion, ham, and butter in a baking pan and mix well. Place the pan directly in the pot.
3. Close the hood and AIR CRISP for 1 minute. Stir and continue to cook for an additional 4 to 5 minutes until the veggies are softened.
4. Meanwhile, whisk together the eggs, milk, and salt in a bowl.
5. Pour the egg mixture over the veggie mixture.
6. Reduce the grill temperature to 360°F and BAKE for 13 to 15 minutes more, or until the top is lightly golden browned and the eggs are set.
7. Scatter the omelet with the shredded cheese. Bake for another 1 minute until the cheese has melted.
8. Let the omelet cool for 5 minutes before serving.

Grilled Sausage Mix

Servings: 4
Cooking Time: 22 Minutes
Ingredients:
- 8 mini bell peppers
- 2 heads radicchio, each cut into 6 wedges
- Canola oil, for brushing
- Sea salt, to taste
- Freshly ground black pepper, to taste
- 6 breakfast sausage links
- 6 hot or sweet Italian sausage links

Directions:
1. Insert the Grill Grate and close the hood. Select GRILL, set the temperature to MAX, and set the time to 22 minutes. Select START/STOP to begin preheating.
2. While the unit is preheating, brush the bell peppers and radicchio with the oil. Season with salt and black pepper.
3. When the unit beeps to signify it has preheated, place the bell peppers and radicchio on the Grill Grate; close the hood and GRILL for 10 minutes, without flipping.
4. Meanwhile, poke the sausages with a fork or knife and brush them with some of the oil.
5. After 10 minutes, remove the vegetables and set aside. Decrease the temperature to LOW. Place the sausages on the Grill Grate; close the hood and GRILL for 6 minutes.
6. Flip the sausages. Close the hood and GRILL for 6 minutes more. Remove the sausages from the Grill Grate.
7. Serve the sausages and vegetables on a large cutting board or serving tray.

Tomato-corn Frittata With Avocado Dressing

Servings: 2 Or 3
Cooking Time: 20 Minutes
Ingredients:

- ½ cup cherry tomatoes, halved
- Kosher salt and freshly ground black pepper, to taste
- 6 large eggs, lightly beaten
- ½ cup corn kernels, thawed if frozen
- ¼ cup milk
- 1 tablespoon finely chopped fresh dill
- ½ cup shredded Monterey Jack cheese
- Avocado Dressing:
- 1 ripe avocado, pitted and peeled
- 2 tablespoons fresh lime juice
- ¼ cup olive oil
- 1 scallion, finely chopped
- 8 fresh basil leaves, finely chopped

Directions:

1. Put the tomato halves in a colander and lightly season with salt. Set aside for 10 minutes to drain well. Pour the tomatoes into a large bowl and fold in the eggs, corn, milk, and dill. Sprinkle with salt and pepper and stir until mixed.
2. Select BAKE, set the temperature to 300ºF, and set the time to 20 minutes. Select START/STOP to begin preheating.
3. Pour the egg mixture into a baking pan. Place the pan directly in the pot. Close the hood and BAKE for 15 minutes.
4. Scatter the cheese on top. Increase the grill temperature to 315ºF and continue to cook for another 5 minutes, or until the frittata is puffy and set.
5. Meanwhile, make the avocado dressing: Mash the avocado with the lime juice in a medium bowl until smooth. Mix in the olive oil, scallion, and basil and stir until well incorporated.
6. Let the frittata cool for 5 minutes and serve alongside the avocado dressing.

Bacon And Egg Stuffed Peppers

Servings: 4
Cooking Time: 15 Minutes
Ingredients:

- 1 cup shredded Cheddar cheese
- 4 slices bacon, cooked and chopped
- 4 bell peppers, seeded and tops removed
- 4 large eggs
- Sea salt, to taste
- Freshly ground black pepper, to taste
- Chopped fresh parsley, for garnish

Directions:

1. Insert the Crisper Basket and close the hood. Select AIR CRISP, set the temperature to 390ºF, and set the time to 15 minutes. Select START/STOP to begin preheating.
2. Meanwhile, divide the cheese and bacon between the bell peppers. Crack one of the eggs into each bell pepper, and season with salt and pepper.
3. When the unit beeps to signify it has preheated, place each bell pepper in the basket. Close the hood and AIR CRISP for 10 to 15 minutes, until the egg whites are cooked and the yolks are slightly runny.
4. Remove the peppers from the basket, garnish with parsley, and serve.

Stuffed Bell Peppers With Italian Maple-glazed Sausage

Servings: 6
Cooking Time: 28 Minutes
Ingredients:
- 2 pounds ground Italian sausage or links
- 1 cup light brown sugar, packed
- 6 bell peppers (any color)
- 1 cup water
- 12 tablespoons (¾ cup) maple syrup, divided

Directions:
1. Insert the Cooking Pot and close the hood. Select GRILL, set the temperature to HI, and set the time to 8 minutes. Select START/STOP to begin preheating.
2. While the unit is preheating, remove the sausage from the casings if using links.
3. When the unit beeps to signify it has preheated, place the sausage and brown sugar in the Cooking Pot. Use a wooden spoon or potato masher to break the sausage apart and mix it with the brown sugar. Close the hood and cook for 8 minutes.
4. While the sausage is cooking, cut the top off each bell pepper and remove the seeds. Then slice the bell peppers in half lengthwise.
5. When cooking is complete, spoon the sausage into each bell pepper cup. Add the water to the Cooking Pot. Place 6 bell pepper halves on the Grill Grate, and place the Grill Grate in the unit.
6. Select GRILL, set the temperature to HI, and set the time to 20 minutes. Select START/STOP and then press the PREHEAT button to skip preheating. Close the hood and cook for 5 minutes.
7. After 5 minutes, open the hood and drizzle 1 tablespoon of maple syrup in each bell pepper cup. Close the hood and cook 5 minutes more. After 5 minutes, remove the stuffed peppers and place the remaining 6 stuffed peppers on the Grill Grate. Repeat this step to cook.
8. When cooking is complete, remove the peppers from the grill and serve.
9. Adding raw sausage inside a bell pepper will result in a watery mess.

Crustless Broccoli Quiche

Servings: 4
Cooking Time: 10 Minutes
Ingredients:
- 1 cup broccoli florets
- ¾ cup chopped roasted red peppers
- 1¼ cups grated Fontina cheese
- 6 eggs
- ¾ cup heavy cream
- ½ teaspoon salt
- Freshly ground black pepper, to taste
- Cooking spray

Directions:
1. Select AIR CRISP, set the temperature to 325°F, and set the time to 10 minutes. Select START/STOP to begin preheating.
2. Spritz a baking pan with cooking spray
3. Add the broccoli florets and roasted red peppers to the pan and scatter the grated Fontina cheese on top.
4. In a bowl, beat together the eggs and heavy cream. Sprinkle with salt and pepper. Pour the egg mixture over the top of the cheese. Wrap the pan in foil.
5. Place the pan directly in the pot. Close the hood and AIR CRISP for 8 minutes. Remove the foil and continue to cook another 2 minutes until the quiche is golden brown.
6. Rest for 5 minutes before cutting into wedges and serve warm.

Bacon And Broccoli Bread Pudding

Servings: 2 To 4
Cooking Time: 48 Minutes
Ingredients:
- ½ pound thick cut bacon, cut into ¼-inch pieces
- 3 cups brioche bread, cut into ½-inch cubes
- 2 tablespoons butter, melted
- 3 eggs
- 1 cup milk
- ½ teaspoon salt
- Freshly ground black pepper, to taste
- 1 cup frozen broccoli florets, thawed and chopped
- 1½ cups grated Swiss cheese

Directions:
1. Insert the Crisper Basket and close the hood. Select AIR CRISP, set the temperature to 400°F, and set the time to 10 minutes. Select START/STOP to begin preheating.
2. Put the bacon in the basket. Close the hood and AIR CRISP for 8 minutes until crispy, shaking the basket a few times to help it cook evenly. Remove the bacon and set it aside on a paper towel.
3. AIR CRISP the brioche bread cubes for 2 minutes to dry and toast lightly.
4. Butter a cake pan. Combine all the remaining ingredients in a large bowl and toss well. Transfer the mixture to the buttered cake pan, cover with aluminum foil and refrigerate the bread pudding overnight, or for at least 8 hours.
5. Remove the cake pan from the refrigerator an hour before you plan to bake and let it sit on the countertop to come to room temperature.
6. Select BAKE, set the temperature to 330°F, and set the time to 40 minutes. Select START/STOP to begin preheating.
7. Place the covered cake pan directly in the pot. Fold the ends of the aluminum foil over the top of the pan. Close the hood and BAKE for 20 minutes. Remove the foil and bake for an additional 20 minutes. If the top browns a little too much before the custard has set, simply return the foil to the pan. The bread pudding has cooked through when a skewer inserted into the center comes out clean.
8. Serve warm.

Pesto Egg Croissantwiches

Servings: 4
Cooking Time: 8 Minutes
Ingredients:
- 4 large eggs
- 4 croissants
- 8 tablespoons pesto

Directions:
1. Insert the Cooking Pot and close the hood. Select GRILL, set the temperature to HI, and set the time to 8 minutes. Select START/STOP to begin preheating.
2. While the unit is preheating, in a small bowl, whisk together the eggs.
3. When the unit beeps to signify it has preheated, pour the beaten eggs into the Cooking Pot. Close the hood and cook for 4 minutes.
4. While the eggs are cooking, split the croissants. Place the croissant halves on top of the Grill Grate.
5. After 4 minutes, open the hood and scramble the eggs with a spatula. Spoon the scrambled eggs onto the bottom halves of the croissants. Remove the Cooking Pot from the unit.
6. Insert the Grill Grate into the unit. Spoon 2 tablespoons of pesto on top of each egg-topped croissant, then top each sandwich with the croissant top. Close the hood and cook for 4 minutes.
7. When cooking is complete, the croissant crust should be toasted. Serve.

Breakfast Tater Tot Casserole

Servings: 4
Cooking Time: 17 To 19 Minutes

Ingredients:

- 4 eggs
- 1 cup milk
- Salt and pepper, to taste
- 12 ounces ground chicken sausage
- 1 pound frozen tater tots, thawed
- ¾ cup grated Cheddar cheese
- Cooking spray

Directions:

1. Whisk together the eggs and milk in a medium bowl. Season with salt and pepper to taste and stir until mixed. Set aside.
2. Place a skillet over medium-high heat and spritz with cooking spray. Place the ground sausage in the skillet and break it into smaller pieces with a spatula or spoon. Cook for 3 to 4 minutes until the sausage starts to brown, stirring occasionally. Remove from heat and set aside.
3. Select BAKE, set the temperature to 400°F, and set the time to 15 minutes. Select START/STOP to begin preheating.
4. Coat a baking pan with cooking spray.
5. Arrange the tater tots in the baking pan. Place the pan directly in the pot. Close the hood and BAKE for 15 minutes. Stir in the egg mixture and cooked sausage. Bake for another 6 minutes.
6. Scatter the cheese on top of the tater tots. Continue to bake for 2 to 3 minutes more until the cheese is bubbly and melted.
7. Let the mixture cool for 5 minutes and serve warm.

Blueberry Dump Cake

Servings: 6 To 8
Cooking Time: 25 Minutes

Ingredients:

- 3 cups fresh blueberries
- ½ cup granulated sugar
- 1 (16-ounce) box yellow cake mix
- 8 tablespoons (1 stick) unsalted butter, melted

Directions:

1. Select BAKE, set the temperature to 300°F, and set the time to 25 minutes. Select START/STOP to begin preheating.
2. While the unit is preheating, wash and pat dry the blueberries. Then place them and the sugar into the Cooking Pot and mix to coat the fruit with the sugar.
3. In a large bowl, mix together the cake mix and melted butter. Stir until the cake mix is no longer a powder but crumbly like a streusel. Cover the blueberry-sugar mixture with the cake crumble.
4. When the unit beeps to signify it has preheated, place the Cooking Pot in the unit. Close the hood and bake for 25 minutes.
5. Baking is complete when the fresh blueberries have bubbled and the cake crumble is golden brown. Serve.

Grilled Kielbasa And Pineapple Kebabs

Servings: 4
Cooking Time: 12 Minutes
Ingredients:

- ½ cup soy sauce
- ¼ cup light brown sugar, packed
- 2 (8-ounce) cans pineapple chunks, drained
- 2 (12-ounce) packages kielbasa sausages, cut into ½-inch slices

Directions:

1. In a large bowl, mix together the soy sauce, brown sugar, and pineapple chunks until the sugar is dissolved. Add the sausage slices and set aside for 10 minutes.
2. Thread the kielbasa and pineapple onto 10 to 12 skewers, alternating meat and fruit. Set aside any glaze that remains in the bowl.
3. Insert the Grill Grate and close the hood. Select GRILL, set the temperature to HI, and set the time to 12 minutes. Select START/STOP to begin preheating.
4. When the unit beeps to signify it has preheated, place half of the skewers on the Grill Grate. Brush them with extra glaze. Close the hood and grill for 3 minutes.
5. After 3 minutes, open the hood and flip the skewers. Close the hood and cook for 3 minutes more. After a total of 6 minutes, remove the skewers. Repeat with the remaining skewers.
6. When cooking is complete, remove the skewers from the grill and serve.

Breakfast Chilaquiles

Servings: 4
Cooking Time: 15 Minutes
Ingredients:

- 4 cups tortilla chips (40 to 50 chips)
- 1 (10- to 14-ounce) can red chile sauce or enchilada sauce
- 6 large eggs
- ¼ cup diced onion, for garnish
- ½ cup crumbled queso fresco, for garnish
- Chopped fresh cilantro, for garnish

Directions:

1. Select GRILL, set the temperature to HI, and set the time to 15 minutes. Select START/STOP to begin preheating.
2. While the unit is preheating, add the tortilla chips to the Cooking Pot and pour the red chile sauce over them.
3. When the unit beeps to signify it has preheated, place the Cooking Pot in the unit. Crack the eggs, one at a time, over the tortilla chips, making sure they're evenly spread out. Close the hood and cook for 15 minutes.
4. Cooking is complete when the egg whites are firm with a runny yellow center. Garnish with the onion, queso fresco, and fresh cilantro, and serve.

Asparagus And Cheese Strata

Servings: 4
Cooking Time: 14 To 19 Minutes
Ingredients:

- 6 asparagus spears, cut into 2-inch pieces
- 1 tablespoon water
- 2 slices whole-wheat bread, cut into ½-inch cubes
- 4 eggs
- 3 tablespoons whole milk
- 2 tablespoons chopped flat-leaf parsley
- ½ cup grated Havarti or Swiss cheese
- Pinch salt
- Freshly ground black pepper, to taste
- Cooking spray

Directions:

1. Select BAKE, set the temperature to 330ºF, and set the time to 19 minutes. Select START/STOP to begin preheating.
2. Add the asparagus spears and 1 tablespoon of water in a baking pan. Place the pan directly in the pot. Close the hood and BAKE for 3 to 5 minutes until crisp-tender. Remove the asparagus from the pan and drain on paper towels. Spritz the pan with cooking spray.
3. Place the bread and asparagus in the pan.
4. Whisk together the eggs and milk in a medium mixing bowl until creamy. Fold in the parsley, cheese, salt, and pepper and stir to combine. Pour this mixture into the baking pan.
5. Place the pan directly in the pot. Close the hood and BAKE for 11 to 14 minutes, or until the eggs are set and the top is lightly browned.
6. Let cool for 5 minutes before slicing and serving.

Everything Bagel Breakfast Bake

Servings: 4
Cooking Time: 25 Minutes
Ingredients:

- 6 large eggs
- 2 cups milk
- ½ cup heavy (whipping) cream
- 4 everything bagels, cut into 1-inch cubes (or bagel flavor of choice)
- 2 cups cherry tomatoes
- 1 pound cream cheese, cut into cubes

Directions:

1. In a large bowl, whisk together the eggs, milk, and heavy cream.
2. Add the bagel cubes to the egg mixture. Set aside to rest for 25 minutes.
3. After 25 minutes, insert the Cooking Pot and close the hood. Select BAKE, set the temperature to 375ºF, and set the time to 25 minutes. Select START/STOP to begin preheating.
4. While the unit is preheating, slice the cherry tomatoes into thirds.
5. When the unit beeps to signify it has preheated, pour the bagel mixture into the Cooking Pot. Top with the sliced cherry tomatoes and evenly place the cream cheese cubes over the top. Close the hood and bake for 25 minutes.
6. When cooking is complete, remove the pot from the grill and serve.

Egg And Avocado Burrito

Servings: 4

Cooking Time: 3 To 5 Minutes

Ingredients:

- 4 low-sodium whole-wheat flour tortillas
- Filling:
- 1 hard-boiled egg, chopped
- 2 hard-boiled egg whites, chopped
- 1 ripe avocado, peeled, pitted, and chopped
- 1 red bell pepper, chopped
- 1 slice low-sodium, low-fat American cheese, torn into pieces
- 3 tablespoons low-sodium salsa, plus additional for serving (optional)

Directions:

1. Insert the Crisper Basket and close the hood. Select AIR CRISP, set the temperature to 390°F, and set the time to 5 minutes. Select START/STOP to begin preheating.

2. Make the filling: Combine the egg, egg whites, avocado, red bell pepper, cheese, and salsa in a medium bowl and stir until blended.

3. Assemble the burritos: Arrange the tortillas on a clean work surface and place ¼ of the prepared filling in the middle of each tortilla, leaving about 1½-inch on each end unfilled. Fold in the opposite sides of each tortilla and roll up. Secure with toothpicks through the center, if needed.

4. Transfer the burritos to the Crisper Basket. Close the hood and AIR CRISP for 3 to 5 minutes, or until the burritos are crisp and golden brown.

5. Allow to cool for 5 minutes and serve with salsa, if desired.

Fried Potatoes With Peppers And Onions

Servings: 4

Cooking Time: 35 Minutes

Ingredients:

- 1 pound red potatoes, cut into ½-inch dices
- 1 large red bell pepper, cut into ½-inch dices
- 1 large green bell pepper, cut into ½-inch dices
- 1 medium onion, cut into ½-inch dices
- 1½ tablespoons extra-virgin olive oil
- 1¼ teaspoons kosher salt
- ¾ teaspoon sweet paprika
- ¾ teaspoon garlic powder
- Freshly ground black pepper, to taste

Directions:

1. Insert the Crisper Basket and close the hood. Select AIR CRISP, set the temperature to 350°F, and set the time to 35 minutes. Select START/STOP to begin preheating.

2. Mix together the potatoes, bell peppers, onion, oil, salt, paprika, garlic powder, and black pepper in a large mixing and toss to coat.

3. Transfer the potato mixture to the Crisper Basket. Close the hood and AIR CRISP for 35 minutes, or until the potatoes are nicely browned. Shake the basket three times during cooking.

4. Remove from the basket to a plate and serve warm.

Banana Chips With Peanut Butter

Servings: 1
Cooking Time: 8 Hours
Ingredients:
- 2 bananas, sliced into ¼-inch rounds
- 2 tablespoons creamy peanut butter

Directions:
1. In a medium bowl, toss the banana slices with the peanut butter, until well coated. If the peanut butter is too thick and not mixing well, add 1 to 2 tablespoons of water.
2. Place the banana slices flat on the Crisper Basket. Arrange them in a single layer, without any slices touching each another.
3. Place the basket in the pot and close the hood.
4. Select DEHYDRATE, set the temperature to 135°F, and set the time to 8 hours. Select START/STOP.
5. When cooking is complete, remove the basket from the pot. Transfer the banana chips to an airtight container and store at room temperature.

Egg And Sausage Stuffed Breakfast Pockets

Servings: 4
Cooking Time: 23 Minutes
Ingredients:
- 1 package ground breakfast sausage, crumbled
- 3 large eggs, lightly beaten
- ⅓ cup diced red bell pepper
- ⅓ cup thinly sliced scallions (green part only)
- Sea salt, to taste
- Freshly ground black pepper, to taste
- 1 package pizza dough
- All-purpose flour, for dusting
- 1 cup shredded Cheddar cheese
- 2 tablespoons canola oil

Directions:
1. Select ROAST, set the temperature to 375°F, and set the time to 15 minutes. Select START/STOP to begin preheating.
2. When the unit beeps to signify it has preheated, place the sausage directly in the pot. Close the hood, and ROAST for 10 minutes, checking the sausage every 2 to 3 minutes, breaking apart larger pieces with a wooden spoon.
3. After 10 minutes, pour the eggs, bell pepper, and scallions into the pot. Stir to evenly incorporate with the sausage. Close the hood and let the eggs roast for the remaining 5 minutes, stirring occasionally. Transfer the sausage and egg mixture to a medium bowl to cool slightly. Season with salt and pepper.
4. Insert the Crisper Basket and close the hood. Select AIR CRISP, set the temperature to 350°F, and set the time to 8 minutes. Select START/STOP to begin preheating.
5. Meanwhile, divide the dough into four equal pieces. Lightly dust a clean work surface with flour. Roll each piece of dough into a 5-inch round of even thickness. Divide the sausage-egg mixture and cheese evenly among each round. Brush the outside edge of the dough with water. Fold the dough over the filling, forming a half circle. Pinch the edges of the dough together to seal in the filling. Brush both sides of each pocket with the oil.
6. When the unit beeps to signify it has preheated, place the breakfast pockets in the basket. Close the hood and AIR CRISP for 6 to 8 minutes, or until golden brown.

Spinach Omelet

Servings: 1

Cooking Time: 10 Minutes

Ingredients:

- 1 teaspoon olive oil
- 3 eggs
- Salt and ground black pepper, to taste
- 1 tablespoon ricotta cheese
- ¼ cup chopped spinach
- 1 tablespoon chopped parsley

Directions:

1. Grease a baking pan with olive oil.
2. Select BAKE, set the temperature to 330°F, and set the time to 10 minutes. Select START/STOP to begin preheating.
3. In a bowl, beat the eggs with a fork and sprinkle salt and pepper.
4. Add the ricotta, spinach, and parsley and then transfer to the baking pan. Place the pan directly in the pot.
5. Close the hood and BAKE for 10 minutes or until the egg is set.
6. Serve warm.

Olives, Kale, And Pecorino Baked Eggs

Servings: 2

Cooking Time: 10 To 12 Minutes

Ingredients:

- 1 cup roughly chopped kale leaves, stems and center ribs removed
- ¼ cup grated pecorino cheese
- ¼ cup olive oil
- 1 garlic clove, peeled
- 3 tablespoons whole almonds
- Kosher salt and freshly ground black pepper, to taste
- 4 large eggs
- 2 tablespoons heavy cream
- 3 tablespoons chopped pitted mixed olives

Directions:

1. Place the kale, pecorino, olive oil, garlic, almonds, salt, and pepper in a small blender and blitz until well incorporated.
2. Select BAKE, set the temperature to 300°F, and set the time to 12 minutes. Select START/STOP to begin preheating.
3. One at a time, crack the eggs in a baking pan. Drizzle the kale pesto on top of the egg whites. Top the yolks with the cream and swirl together the yolks and the pesto.
4. Place the pan directly in the pot. Close the hood and BAKE for 10 to 12 minutes, or until the top begins to brown and the eggs are set.
5. Allow the eggs to cool for 5 minutes. Scatter the olives on top and serve warm.

Cornflakes Toast Sticks

Servings: 4
Cooking Time: 6 Minutes

Ingredients:

- 2 eggs
- ½ cup milk
- ⅛ teaspoon salt
- ½ teaspoon pure vanilla extract
- ¾ cup crushed cornflakes
- 6 slices sandwich bread, each slice cut into 4 strips
- Maple syrup, for dipping
- Cooking spray

Directions:

1. Insert the Crisper Basket and close the hood. Select AIR CRISP, set the temperature to 390°F, and set the time to 6 minutes. Select START/STOP to begin preheating.
2. In a small bowl, beat together the eggs, milk, salt, and vanilla.
3. Put crushed cornflakes on a plate or in a shallow dish.
4. Dip bread strips in egg mixture, shake off excess, and roll in cornflake crumbs.
5. Spray both sides of bread strips with oil.
6. Put bread strips in Crisper Basket in a single layer.
7. Close the hood and AIR CRISP for 6 minutes or until golden brown.
8. Repeat steps 5 and 6 to AIR CRISP remaining French toast sticks.
9. Serve with maple syrup.

Avocado Eggs

Servings: 4
Cooking Time: 10 Minutes

Ingredients:

- 4 ripe avocados, divided
- 3 tablespoons extra-virgin olive oil
- 1 teaspoon salt
- ½ teaspoon freshly ground black pepper
- 8 small eggs
- Hot sauce or salsa, for garnish (optional)

Directions:

1. Insert the Grill Grate and close the hood. Select GRILL, set the temperature to HI, and set the time to 10 minutes. Select START/STOP to begin preheating.
2. While the unit is preheating, cut the avocados in half lengthwise and remove the pits, but leave the skin on. You may need to scoop out some of the green flesh so the egg fits once added. Set the extra flesh aside to use as an additional topping later.
3. In a small bowl, whisk together the olive oil, salt, and pepper. Brush the seasoned olive oil on the flesh of the avocados. Then, crack an egg into the center of each avocado half.
4. When the unit beeps to signify it has preheated, place the avocados on the grill, egg-side up. Close the hood and grill for 10 minutes.
5. Cooking is complete when the egg whites are firm. Remove the avocados from the grill. Garnish with the reserved avocado and top with your favorite hot sauce or salsa, if desired.

Mushroom And Squash Toast

Servings: 4

Cooking Time: 10 Minutes

Ingredients:

- 1 tablespoon olive oil
- 1 red bell pepper, cut into strips
- 2 green onions, sliced
- 1 cup sliced button or cremini mushrooms
- 1 small yellow squash, sliced
- 2 tablespoons softened butter
- 4 slices bread
- ½ cup soft goat cheese

Directions:

1. Brush the Crisper Basket with the olive oil.

2. Insert the Crisper Basket and close the hood. Select AIR CRISP, set the temperature to 350°F, and set the time to 7 minutes. Select START/STOP to begin preheating.

3. Put the red pepper, green onions, mushrooms, and squash inside the basket and give them a stir. Close the hood and AIR CRISP for 7 minutes or the vegetables are tender, shaking the basket once throughout the cooking time.

4. Remove the vegetables and set them aside.

5. Spread the butter on the slices of bread and transfer to the basket, butter-side up. Close the hood and AIR CRISP for 3 minutes.

6. Remove the toast from the grill and top with goat cheese and vegetables. Serve warm.

Supersized Family Pizza Omelet

Servings: 4

Cooking Time: 10 Minutes

Ingredients:

- 10 large eggs
- 1 tablespoon Italian seasoning
- ½ cup pizza or marinara sauce
- 1 cup shredded mozzarella cheese
- 2 ounces pepperoni slices (about 24 slices)

Directions:

1. Insert the Cooking Pot and close the hood. Select GRILL, set the temperature to HI, and set the time to 10 minutes. Select START/STOP to begin preheating.

2. While the unit is preheating, in a medium bowl, whisk together the eggs and Italian seasoning.

3. When the unit beeps to signify it has preheated, pour the egg mixture into the Cooking Pot. Close the hood and cook for 5 minutes.

4. Place the Grill Grate next to the unit on top of the counter. After 5 minutes, open the hood and use a spatula to fold the egg sheet in half, then place it on top of the Grill Grate.

5. Place the Grill Grate into the unit. Top the omelet with the pizza sauce, mozzarella cheese, and pepperoni slices. Close the hood and cook for 5 minutes more.

6. When cooking is complete, the cheese will be melted. Remove the omelet from the grill and serve.

Egg And Bacon Nests

Servings:12
Cooking Time: 30 Minutes
Ingredients:
- 3 tablespoons avocado oil
- 12 slices bacon
- 12 eggs
- Salt
- Freshly ground black pepper

Directions:
1. Insert the Grill Grate and close the hood. Select GRILL, set the temperature to HI, and set the time to 30 minutes. Select START/STOP to begin preheating.
2. While the unit is preheating, brush the avocado oil in the bottom and on the sides of two 6-cup muffin tins. Wrap a bacon slice around the inside of each muffin cup, then crack an egg into each cup. Season to taste with salt and pepper.
3. When the unit beeps to signify it has preheated, place one muffin tin in the center of the Grill Grate. Close the hood and grill for 15 minutes.
4. After 15 minutes, remove the muffin tin. Place the second muffin tin in the center of the Grill Grate, close the hood, and grill for 15 minutes.
5. Serve immediately or let cool and store in resealable bags in the refrigerator for up to 4 days.

Apple And Walnut Muffins

Servings:8
Cooking Time: 10 Minutes
Ingredients:
- 1 cup flour
- ⅓ cup sugar
- 1 teaspoon baking powder
- ¼ teaspoon baking soda
- ¼ teaspoon salt
- 1 teaspoon cinnamon
- ¼ teaspoon ginger
- ¼ teaspoon nutmeg
- 1 egg
- 2 tablespoons pancake syrup, plus 2 teaspoons
- 2 tablespoons melted butter, plus 2 teaspoons
- ¾ cup unsweetened applesauce
- ½ teaspoon vanilla extract
- ¼ cup chopped walnuts
- ¼ cup diced apple

Directions:
1. Select BAKE, set the temperature to 330°F, and set the time to 10 minutes. Select START/STOP to begin preheating.
2. In a large bowl, stir together the flour, sugar, baking powder, baking soda, salt, cinnamon, ginger, and nutmeg.
3. In a small bowl, beat egg until frothy. Add syrup, butter, applesauce, and vanilla and mix well.
4. Pour egg mixture into dry ingredients and stir just until moistened.
5. Gently stir in nuts and diced apple.
6. Divide batter among 8 parchment paper-lined muffin cups.
7. Put 4 muffin cups in the pot. Close the hood and BAKE for 10 minutes.
8. Repeat with remaining 4 muffins or until toothpick inserted in center comes out clean.
9. Serve warm.

Nut And Seed Muffins

Servings:8
Cooking Time: 10 Minutes

Ingredients:

- ½ cup whole-wheat flour, plus 2 tablespoons
- ¼ cup oat bran
- 2 tablespoons flaxseed meal
- ¼ cup brown sugar
- ½ teaspoon baking soda
- ½ teaspoon baking powder
- ¼ teaspoon salt
- ½ teaspoon cinnamon
- ½ cup buttermilk
- 2 tablespoons melted butter
- 1 egg
- ½ teaspoon pure vanilla extract
- ½ cup grated carrots
- ¼ cup chopped pecans
- ¼ cup chopped walnuts
- 1 tablespoon pumpkin seeds
- 1 tablespoon sunflower seeds
- Cooking spray

Directions:

1. Select BAKE, set the temperature to 330°F, and set the time to 10 minutes. Select START/STOP to begin preheating.
2. In a large bowl, stir together the flour, bran, flaxseed meal, sugar, baking soda, baking powder, salt, and cinnamon.
3. In a medium bowl, beat together the buttermilk, butter, egg, and vanilla. Pour into flour mixture and stir just until dry ingredients moisten. Do not beat.
4. Gently stir in carrots, nuts, and seeds.
5. Double up the foil cups so you have 8 total and spritz with cooking spray.
6. Put 4 foil cups in the pot and divide half the batter among them.
7. Close the hood and BAKE for 10 minutes, or until a toothpick inserted in center comes out clean.
8. Repeat step 7 to bake remaining 4 muffins.
9. Serve warm.

Meats Recipes

Potato And Prosciutto Salad

Servings: 8
Cooking Time: 7 Minutes
Ingredients:
- Salad:
- 4 pounds potatoes, boiled and cubed
- 15 slices prosciutto, diced
- 2 cups shredded Cheddar cheese
- Dressing:
- 15 ounces sour cream
- 2 tablespoons mayonnaise
- 1 teaspoon salt
- 1 teaspoon black pepper
- 1 teaspoon dried basil

Directions:
1. Select AIR CRISP, set the temperature to 350°F, and set the time to 7 minutes. Select START/STOP to begin preheating.
2. Put the potatoes, prosciutto, and Cheddar in a baking pan. Place the pan directly in the pot. Close the hood and AIR CRISP for 7 minutes.
3. In a separate bowl, mix the sour cream, mayonnaise, salt, pepper, and basil using a whisk.
4. Coat the salad with the dressing and serve.

Fast Lamb Satay

Servings: 2
Cooking Time: 8 Minutes
Ingredients:
- ¼ teaspoon cumin
- 1 teaspoon ginger
- ½ teaspoons nutmeg
- Salt and ground black pepper, to taste
- 2 boneless lamb steaks
- Cooking spray

Directions:
1. Combine the cumin, ginger, nutmeg, salt and pepper in a bowl.
2. Cube the lamb steaks and massage the spice mixture into each one.
3. Leave to marinate for 10 minutes, then transfer onto metal skewers.
4. Insert the Crisper Basket and close the hood. Select AIR CRISP, set the temperature to 400°F, and set the time to 8 minutes. Select START/STOP to begin preheating.
5. Place the skewers in the basket and spritz with cooking spray. Close the hood and AIR CRISP for 8 minutes.
6. Take care when removing them from the grill and serve.

Steak And Lettuce Salad

Servings: 4 To 6
Cooking Time: 16 Minutes

Ingredients:

- 4 skirt steaks
- Sea salt, to taste
- Freshly ground black pepper, to taste
- 6 cups chopped romaine lettuce
- ¾ cup cherry tomatoes, halved
- ¼ cup blue cheese, crumbled
- 1 cup croutons
- 2 avocados, peeled and sliced
- 1 cup blue cheese dressing

Directions:

1. Insert the Grill Grate and close the hood. Select GRILL, set the temperature to HIGH, and set the time to 8 minutes. Select START/STOP to begin preheating.
2. Season the steaks on both sides with the salt and pepper.
3. When the unit beeps to signify it has preheated, place 2 steaks on the Grill Grate. Gently press the steaks down to maximize grill marks. Close the hood and GRILL for 4 minutes. After 4 minutes, flip the steaks, close the hood, and GRILL for an additional 4 minutes.
4. Remove the steaks from the grill and transfer to them a cutting board. Tent with aluminum foil.
5. Repeat step 3 with the remaining 2 steaks.
6. While the second set of steaks is cooking, assemble the salad by tossing together the lettuce, tomatoes, blue cheese crumbles, and croutons. Top with the avocado slices.
7. Once the second set of steaks has finished cooking, slice all four of the steaks into thin strips, and place on top of the salad. Drizzle with the blue cheese dressing and serve.

Cheesy Beef Meatballs

Servings: 6
Cooking Time: 18 Minutes

Ingredients:

- 1 pound ground beef
- ½ cup grated Parmesan cheese
- 1 tablespoon minced garlic
- ½ cup Mozzarella cheese
- 1 teaspoon freshly ground pepper

Directions:

1. Insert the Crisper Basket and close the hood. Select AIR CRISP, set the temperature to 400°F, and set the time to 18 minutes. Select START/STOP to begin preheating.
2. In a bowl, mix all the ingredients together.
3. Roll the meat mixture into 5 generous meatballs. Transfer to the basket.
4. Close the hood and AIR CRISP for 18 minutes.
5. Serve immediately.

Crusted Pork Chops With Honey-maple Jalapeño Glaze

Servings: 6
Cooking Time: 15 Minutes
Ingredients:

- 2 large eggs
- 2 cups panko bread crumbs
- 1 teaspoon Italian seasoning
- 1 teaspoon garlic powder
- 6 (6-ounce) boneless pork chops
- ¼ cup honey
- ¼ cup maple syrup
- ¼ cup soy sauce
- 1 jalapeño, sliced (seeds optional)

Directions:

1. Insert the Grill Grate and close the hood. Select GRILL, set the temperature to MED, and set the time to 15 minutes. Select START/STOP to begin preheating.
2. While the unit is preheating, create an assembly line with 2 large bowls. In one bowl, whisk the eggs. In the other bowl, combine the panko bread crumbs, Italian seasoning, and garlic powder. One at a time, dip the pork chops in the egg and then in the panko mixture until fully coated and set aside.
3. In a small bowl, combine the honey, maple syrup, soy sauce, and jalapeño slices.
4. When the unit beeps to signify it has preheated, place the pork chops on the Grill Grate. Close the hood and grill for 7 minutes, 30 seconds.
5. After 7 minutes, 30 seconds, open the hood and flip the pork chops. Spoon half of the honey glaze over the chops. Close the hood and cook for 7 minutes, 30 seconds more.
6. When cooking is complete, remove the pork chops from the grill and drizzle with the remaining glaze. Let the pork chops rest for a few minutes before serving.

Smoky Paprika Pork And Vegetable Kabobs

Servings: 4
Cooking Time: 15 Minutes
Ingredients:

- 1 pound pork tenderloin, cubed
- 1 teaspoon smoked paprika
- Salt and ground black pepper, to taste
- 1 green bell pepper, cut into chunks
- 1 zucchini, cut into chunks
- 1 red onion, sliced
- 1 tablespoon oregano
- Cooking spray

Directions:

1. Spritz the Crisper Basket with cooking spray.
2. Insert the Crisper Basket and close the hood. Select AIR CRISP, set the temperature to 350°F, and set the time to 15 minutes. Select START/STOP to begin preheating.
3. Add the pork to a bowl and season with the smoked paprika, salt and black pepper. Thread the seasoned pork cubes and vegetables alternately onto the soaked skewers.
4. Arrange the skewers in the prepared Crisper Basket and spray with cooking spray.
5. Close the hood and AIR CRISP for 15 minutes, or until the pork is well browned and the vegetables are tender, flipping once halfway through.
6. Transfer the skewers to the serving dishes and sprinkle with oregano. Serve hot.

Herb And Pesto Stuffed Pork Loin

Servings: 8
Cooking Time: 15 Minutes
Ingredients:
- 1 (4-pound) boneless center-cut pork loin
- ½ cup avocado oil
- ½ cup grated Parmesan cheese
- 2 tablespoons finely chopped fresh basil
- 1 tablespoon finely chopped fresh parsley
- 1 tablespoon chopped fresh chives
- ½ teaspoon finely chopped fresh rosemary
- 5 garlic cloves, minced

Directions:
1.   Butterfly the pork loin. You can use the same method as you would for a chicken breast or steak (see here), but because a pork loin is thicker, you can perform this double butterfly technique: Place the boneless, trimmed loin on a cutting board. One-third from the bottom of the loin, slice horizontally from the side (parallel to the cutting board), stopping about ½ inch from the opposite side, and open the flap like a book. Make another horizontal cut from the thicker side of the loin to match the thickness of the first cut, stopping again ½ inch from the edge. Open up the flap to create a rectangular piece of flat meat.
2.   Plug the thermometer into the unit. Insert the Grill Grate and close the hood. Select GRILL, set the temperature to MED, and select PRESET. Use the arrows to the right to select PORK. The unit will default to WELL to cook pork to a safe temperature. Select START/STOP to begin preheating.
3.   While the unit is preheating, in a small bowl, combine the avocado oil, Parmesan cheese, basil, parsley, chives, rosemary, and garlic. Spread the pesto sauce evenly over the cut side of each tenderloin. Starting from a longer side, roll up the pork tightly over the filling. Use toothpicks to secure the ends. Insert the Smart Thermometer into the thickest part of the meat.
4.   When the unit beeps to signify it has preheated, place the loin on the Grill Grate. Close the hood to begin cooking.
5.   When the Foodi™ Grill indicates it's time to flip, open the hood and flip the loin. Close the hood to continue cooking.
6.   When cooking is complete, the Smart Thermometer will indicate that the internal temperature has been reached. Open the hood and remove the loin. Let the meat rest for 10 minutes before slicing in between the toothpicks. Serve.

Pepperoni And Bell Pepper Pockets

Servings: 4
Cooking Time: 8 Minutes
Ingredients:
- 4 bread slices, 1-inch thick
- Olive oil, for misting
- 24 slices pepperoni
- 1 ounce roasted red peppers, drained and patted dry
- 1 ounce Pepper Jack cheese, cut into 4 slices

Directions:
1.   Insert the Crisper Basket and close the hood. Select AIR CRISP, set the temperature to 360°F, and set the time to 8 minutes. Select START/STOP to begin preheating.
2.   Spray both sides of bread slices with olive oil.
3.   Stand slices upright and cut a deep slit in the top to create a pocket (almost to the bottom crust, but not all the way through).
4.   Stuff each bread pocket with 6 slices of pepperoni, a large strip of roasted red pepper, and a slice of cheese.
5.   Put bread pockets in Crisper Basket, standing up. Close the hood and AIR CRISP for 8 minutes, until filling is heated through and bread is lightly browned.
6.   Serve hot.

Balsamic Honey Mustard Lamb Chops

Servings: 4 To 6

Cooking Time: 45 Minutes To 1 Hour

Ingredients:

- ¼ cup avocado oil
- ½ cup balsamic vinegar
- 2 garlic cloves, minced
- 1 teaspoon salt
- ½ teaspoon freshly ground black pepper
- 2 tablespoons honey
- 1 tablespoon yellow mustard
- 1 tablespoon fresh rosemary
- 1 (2- to 3-pound) rack of lamb

Directions:

1. In a large bowl, whisk together the avocado oil, vinegar, garlic, salt, pepper, honey, mustard, and rosemary. Add the lamb and massage and coat all sides of the meat with the marinade. Cover and refrigerate for at least 1 hour.

2. Plug the thermometer into the unit. Insert the Cooking Pot and close the hood. Select ROAST, set the temperature to 350°F, and select PRESET. Use the arrows to the right to select BEEF/ LAMB. The unit will default to WELL to cook lamb to a safe temperature. Insert the Smart Thermometer in the thickest part of the lamb without touching bone. Select START/STOP to begin preheating.

3. When the unit beeps to signify it has preheated, place the rack of lamb in the Cooking Pot. Close the hood to begin cooking.

4. When cooking is complete, the Smart Thermometer will indicate that the specified internal temperature has been reached. Remove the lamb from the pot and serve.

Brown-sugared Ham

Servings: 6 To 8

Cooking Time: 30 Minutes

Ingredients:

- 1 (3-pound) bone-in, fully cooked ham quarter
- 3 tablespoons Dijon mustard
- ¼ cup pineapple juice
- ¼ cup apple cider vinegar
- 1 cup light brown sugar, packed
- 1 teaspoon cinnamon
- ½ teaspoon ground ginger

Directions:

1. Plug the thermometer into the unit. Insert the Cooking Pot and close the hood. Select ROAST, set the temperature to 350°F, then select PRESET. Use the arrows to the right to select PORK. The unit will default to WELL to cook pork to a safe temperature. Insert the Smart Thermometer into the thickest part of the ham. Select START/STOP to begin preheating.

2. While the unit is preheating, score the ham using a sharp knife, creating a diamond pattern on top. Brush on the Dijon mustard.

3. In a small bowl, combine the pineapple juice, vinegar, brown sugar, cinnamon, and ginger.

4. When the unit beeps to signify it has preheated, place the ham in the Cooking Pot. Brush some of the glaze over the entire ham, then pour the rest on top so the glaze can seep into the scores. Close the hood to begin cooking.

5. When cooking is complete, the Smart Thermometer will indicate that the desired temperature has been reached. Remove the ham from the pot and let rest for at least 10 minutes before slicing. Serve.

Spicy Pork With Candy Onions

Servings: 4
Cooking Time: 52 Minutes
Ingredients:

- 2 teaspoons sesame oil
- 1 teaspoon dried sage, crushed
- 1 teaspoon cayenne pepper
- 1 rosemary sprig, chopped
- 1 thyme sprig, chopped
- Sea salt and ground black pepper, to taste
- 2 pounds pork leg roast, scored
- ½ pound candy onions, sliced
- 4 cloves garlic, finely chopped
- 2 chili peppers, minced

Directions:

1. Select AIR CRISP, set the temperature to 400°F, and set the time to 52 minutes. Select START/STOP to begin preheating.
2. In a mixing bowl, combine the sesame oil, sage, cayenne pepper, rosemary, thyme, salt and black pepper until well mixed. In another bowl, place the pork leg and brush with the seasoning mixture.
3. Place the seasoned pork leg in a baking pan. Place the pan directly in the pot. Close the hood and AIR CRISP for 40 minutes, or until lightly browned, flipping halfway through. Add the candy onions, garlic and chili peppers to the pan and AIR CRISP for another 12 minutes.
4. Transfer the pork leg to a plate. Let cool for 5 minutes and slice. Spread the juices left in the pan over the pork and serve warm with the candy onions.

Italian Sausage And Peppers

Servings: 4
Cooking Time: 10 Minutes
Ingredients:

- 1 green bell pepper
- 1 large red onion
- 1 pound ground Italian sausage (not links)
- 1 tablespoon garlic, minced
- 2 tablespoons white wine vinegar

Directions:

1. Insert the Cooking Pot and close the hood. Select GRILL, set the temperature to HI, and set the time to 10 minutes. Select START/STOP to begin preheating.
2. While the unit is preheating, cut the bell pepper into strips and slice the red onion.
3. When the unit beeps to signify it has preheated, place the sausage, garlic, and vinegar in the Cooking Pot. Slowly break apart the sausage using a wooden spoon or a spatula. Close the hood and cook for 5 minutes.
4. After 5 minutes, open the hood and stir the sausage. Add the bell pepper and onion. Close the hood and cook for 5 minutes more.
5. When cooking is complete, stir the sausage, pepper, and onion again. Serve.

Rib Eye Steak With Rosemary Butter

Servings: 4

Cooking Time: 10 Minutes

Ingredients:

- 4 garlic cloves, minced
- 1 teaspoon salt
- 4 tablespoons (½ stick) unsalted butter, at room temperature
- ½ tablespoon chopped fresh rosemary (about 2 sprigs)
- 4 (1-pound) bone-in rib eye steaks

Directions:

1. Plug the thermometer into the unit. Insert the Grill Grate and close the hood. Select GRILL, set the temperature to HI, then select PRESET. Use the arrows to the right to select BEEF, then choose MED (6) or desired doneness. Insert the Smart Thermometer into the thickest part of one of the steaks. Select START/STOP to begin preheating.

2. While the unit is preheating, in a small bowl, combine the garlic, salt, butter, and rosemary to form a butter paste.

3. When the unit beeps to signify it has preheated, place the steaks on the Grill Grate. Close the hood to begin cooking.

4. When the grill indicates it is time to flip, open the hood, flip the steaks, and add 1 tablespoon of the rosemary butter on top of each steak. Close the hood and cook until the Smart Thermometer indicates your desired internal temperature has been reached.

5. When cooking is complete, remove the steaks from the grill and let rest for 5 minutes before slicing against the grain. Serve.

Spicy Pork Chops With Carrots And Mushrooms

Servings: 4

Cooking Time: 15 To 18 Minutes

Ingredients:

- 2 carrots, cut into sticks
- 1 cup mushrooms, sliced
- 2 garlic cloves, minced
- 2 tablespoons olive oil
- 1 pound boneless pork chops
- 1 teaspoon dried oregano
- 1 teaspoon dried thyme
- 1 teaspoon cayenne pepper
- Salt and ground black pepper, to taste
- Cooking spray

Directions:

1. Spritz the Crisper Basket with cooking spray.

2. Insert the Crisper Basket and close the hood. Select AIR CRISP, set the temperature to 360°F, and set the time to 18 minutes. Select START/STOP to begin preheating.

3. In a mixing bowl, toss together the carrots, mushrooms, garlic, olive oil and salt until well combined.

4. Add the pork chops to a different bowl and season with oregano, thyme, cayenne pepper, salt and black pepper.

5. Lower the vegetable mixture in the prepared Crisper Basket. Place the seasoned pork chops on top. Close the hood and AIR CRISP for 15 to 18 minutes, or until the pork is well browned and the vegetables are tender, flipping the pork and shaking the basket once halfway through.

6. Transfer the pork chops to the serving dishes and let cool for 5 minutes. Serve warm with vegetable on the side.

Spicy Beef Lettuce Wraps

Servings: 4
Cooking Time: 10 Minutes
Ingredients:

- 1 pound ground beef
- 1 tablespoon sesame oil
- 1 tablespoon minced garlic
- 1 teaspoon peeled minced fresh ginger
- 3 tablespoons light brown sugar, packed
- ¼ cup soy sauce
- 1 teaspoon salt
- ½ teaspoon freshly ground black pepper
- 2 teaspoons sriracha
- 1 red chile, thinly sliced, or ¼ teaspoon red pepper flakes
- ½ cup sliced scallions, both white and green parts
- 12 butter lettuce leaves

Directions:

1. Insert the Cooking Pot and close the hood. Select GRILL, set the temperature to HI, and set the time to 10 minutes. Select START/STOP to begin preheating.
2. When the unit beeps to signify it has preheated, place the ground beef in the Cooking Pot. Carefully break the ground beef apart with a wooden spoon or spatula. Stir in the sesame oil, garlic, and ginger. Close the hood and cook for 5 minutes.
3. After 5 minutes, open the hood and stir the ground beef. Stir in the brown sugar, soy sauce, salt, pepper, and sriracha. Close the hood and cook for 5 minutes more.
4. When cooking is complete, open the hood and stir in the chile and scallions. Close the hood and let sit for about 3 minutes for the mixture to set.
5. Scoop the ground beef mixture into the lettuce leaves and serve.

Char Siew

Servings: 4 To 6
Cooking Time: 20 Minutes
Ingredients:

- 1 strip of pork shoulder butt with a good amount of fat marbling
- Olive oil, for brushing the pan
- Marinade:
- 1 teaspoon sesame oil
- 4 tablespoons raw honey
- 1 teaspoon low-sodium dark soy sauce
- 1 teaspoon light soy sauce
- 1 tablespoon rose wine
- 2 tablespoons Hoisin sauce

Directions:

1. Combine all the marinade ingredients together in a Ziploc bag. Put pork in bag, making sure all sections of pork strip are engulfed in the marinade. Chill for 3 to 24 hours.
2. Take out the strip 30 minutes before planning to roast.
3. Select ROAST, set the temperature to 350°F, and set the time to 20 minutes. Select START/STOP to begin preheating.
4. Put foil on the pot and brush with olive oil. Put marinated pork strip onto prepared pot.
5. Close the hood and ROAST for 20 minutes.
6. Glaze with marinade every 5 to 10 minutes.
7. Remove strip and leave to cool a few minutes before slicing.
8. Serve immediately.

Green Curry Beef

Servings: 4
Cooking Time: 12 Minutes
Ingredients:
- 1 yellow onion
- 1 red bell pepper
- 2 pounds sirloin steak
- 1 tablespoon minced garlic
- 1 tablespoon light brown sugar, packed
- 2 tablespoons green curry paste
- 1 teaspoon salt
- ½ teaspoon freshly ground black pepper
- Juice of ½ lime
- 1 (13-ounce) can full-fat unsweetened coconut milk
- 2 tablespoons fish sauce (optional)
- 1 cup fresh Thai basil or sweet basil

Directions:
1. Insert the Cooking Pot and close the hood. Select GRILL, set the temperature to MED, and set the time to 12 minutes. Select START/STOP to begin preheating.
2. While the unit is preheating, dice the onion, slice the red bell pepper, and thinly slice the steak into bite-size strips.
3. When the unit beeps to signify it has preheated, place the onion and garlic in the Cooking Pot. Then add the beef and stir with a wooden spoon. Close the hood and cook for 4 minutes.
4. After 4 minutes, open the hood and add the brown sugar, green curry paste, salt, pepper, lime juice, coconut milk, and fish sauce (if using). Close the hood and cook for 4 minutes. After 4 minutes, open the hood and stir the curry. Close the hood and cook for 4 minutes more.
5. When cooking is complete, open the hood, add the basil, and stir one more time. Close the hood and let the coconut curry sit for 5 minutes before serving.

Homemade Teriyaki Pork Ribs

Servings: 4
Cooking Time: 30 Minutes
Ingredients:
- ¼ cup soy sauce
- ¼ cup honey
- 1 teaspoon garlic powder
- 1 teaspoon ground dried ginger
- 4 boneless country-style pork ribs
- Cooking spray

Directions:
1. Spritz the Crisper Basket with cooking spray.
2. Insert the Crisper Basket and close the hood. Select AIR CRISP, set the temperature to 350°F, and set the time to 30 minutes. Select START/STOP to begin preheating.
3. Make the teriyaki sauce: combine the soy sauce, honey, garlic powder, and ginger in a bowl. Stir to mix well.
4. Brush the ribs with half of the teriyaki sauce, then arrange the ribs in the basket. Spritz with cooking spray. You may need to work in batches to avoid overcrowding.
5. Close the hood and AIR CRISP for 30 minutes or until the internal temperature of the ribs reaches at least 145°F. Brush the ribs with remaining teriyaki sauce and flip halfway through.
6. Serve immediately.

Burnt Ends

Servings: 6
Cooking Time: 40 Minutes
Ingredients:
- 1 tablespoon garlic powder
- 1 tablespoon sea salt
- 1 tablespoon paprika
- ¼ teaspoon freshly ground black pepper
- 2 pounds pork butt, cut into 1-inch cubes
- ½ cup barbecue sauce
- ¼ cup light brown sugar, packed
- ¼ cup honey
- 4 tablespoons (½ stick) unsalted butter, sliced

Directions:
1. Insert the Cooking Pot and close the hood. Select ROAST, set the temperature to 300°F, and set the time to 20 minutes. Select START/STOP to begin preheating.
2. While the unit is preheating, in a large bowl, combine the garlic powder, salt, paprika, and pepper. Add the pork and toss until generously coated on all sides.
3. When the unit beeps to signify it has preheated, place the pork in the Cooking Pot in a single layer. Close the hood and roast for 10 minutes.
4. After 10 minutes, open the hood and flip the pork cubes. Close the hood and cook for 10 minutes more.
5. At this point, the pork should have a nice char. Place the pork cubes in the center of a large piece of aluminum foil. Add the barbecue sauce, brown sugar, and honey and massage them into the roasted pork. Add the butter, then seal the foil. Place the packet back in the Cooking Pot.
6. Select ROAST, set the temperature to 350°F, and set the time to 20 minutes. Select START/STOP and then press PREHEAT to skip preheating. Close the hood and cook for 20 minutes.
7. When cooking is complete, remove the foil packet. Be careful opening the foil, because the steam will be very hot. The pork should be nicely coated with sauce that has thickened. If you want more char and caramelization of the burnt ends, carefully place the open foil packet back in the Cooking Pot. Select GRILL, set the temperature to HI, and set the time to 10 minutes. Select START/STOP and then press PREHEAT to skip preheating. Close the hood and cook for 10 minutes or until charred to your liking.

Crispy Pork Belly Bites

Servings: 6
Cooking Time: 20 Minutes
Ingredients:
- 1 tablespoon garlic powder
- 1 tablespoon sea salt
- 1 tablespoon paprika
- ¼ teaspoon freshly ground black pepper
- 2 pounds pork belly (3 to 4 slabs)

Directions:
1. Insert the Grill Grate and close the hood. Select GRILL, set the temperature to HI, and set the time to 20 minutes. Select START/STOP to begin preheating.
2. While the unit is preheating, in a large bowl, combine the garlic powder, salt, paprika, and pepper.
3. Pat the pork belly dry with a paper towel. Place it in the seasoning and toss to generously coat the pork belly on all sides.
4. When the unit beeps to signify it has preheated, place the pork belly on the Grill Grate, skin-side up. Close the hood and grill for 10 minutes.
5. After 10 minutes, open the hood and flip the pork. Close the hood and cook for 10 minutes more.
6. When cooking is complete, remove the pork belly from the grill and serve.

Sausage Ratatouille

Servings: 4
Cooking Time: 25 Minutes
Ingredients:
- 4 pork sausages
- Ratatouille:
- 2 zucchinis, sliced
- 1 eggplant, sliced
- 15 ounces tomatoes, sliced
- 1 red bell pepper, sliced
- 1 medium red onion, sliced
- 1 cup canned butter beans, drained
- 1 tablespoon balsamic vinegar
- 2 garlic cloves, minced
- 1 red chili, chopped
- 2 tablespoons fresh thyme, chopped
- 2 tablespoons olive oil

Directions:
1. Insert the Crisper Basket and close the hood. Select AIR CRISP, set the temperature to 390°F, and set the time to 10 minutes. Select START/STOP to begin preheating.
2. Place the sausages in the basket. Close the hood and AIR CRISP for 10 minutes or until the sausage is lightly browned. Flip the sausages halfway through.
3. Meanwhile, make the ratatouille: arrange the vegetable slices on the a baking pan alternatively, then add the remaining ingredients on top.
4. Transfer the sausage to a plate. Place the pan directly in the pot. Close the hood and BAKE for 15 minutes or until the vegetables are tender.
5. Serve the ratatouille with the sausage on top.

Citrus Carnitas

Servings: 6
Cooking Time: 25 Minutes
Ingredients:
- 2½ pounds boneless country-style pork ribs, cut into 2-inch pieces
- 3 tablespoons olive brine
- 1 tablespoon minced fresh oregano leaves
- ⅓ cup orange juice
- 1 teaspoon ground cumin
- 1 tablespoon minced garlic
- 1 teaspoon salt
- 1 teaspoon ground black pepper
- Cooking spray

Directions:
1. Combine all the ingredients in a large bowl. Toss to coat the pork ribs well. Wrap the bowl in plastic and refrigerate for at least an hour to marinate.
2. Spritz the Crisper Basket with cooking spray.
3. Insert the Crisper Basket and close the hood. Select AIR CRISP, set the temperature to 400°F, and set the time to 25 minutes. Select START/STOP to begin preheating.
4. Arrange the marinated pork ribs in a single layer in the basket and spritz with cooking spray.
5. Close the hood and AIR CRISP for 25 minutes or until well browned. Flip the ribs halfway through.
6. Serve immediately.

Asian-flavored Steak Kebabs

Servings: 4
Cooking Time: 12 Minutes
Ingredients:

- ¾ cup soy sauce
- 5 garlic cloves, minced
- 3 tablespoons sesame oil
- ½ cup canola oil
- ⅓ cup sugar
- ¼ teaspoon dried ground ginger
- 2 New York strip steaks, cut in 2-inch cubes
- 1 cup whole white mushrooms
- 1 red bell pepper, seeded, and cut into 2-inch cubes
- 1 red onion, cut into 2-inch wedges

Directions:

1. In a medium bowl, whisk together the soy sauce, garlic, sesame oil, canola oil, sugar, and ginger until well combined. Add the steak and toss to coat. Cover and refrigerate for at least 30 minutes.

2. Insert the Grill Grate and close the hood. Select GRILL, set the temperature to MEDIUM, and set the time to 12 minutes. Select START/STOP to begin preheating.

3. While the unit is preheating, assemble the skewers in the following order: steak, mushroom, bell pepper, onion. Ensure the ingredients are pushed almost completely down to the end of the wood skewers.

4. When the unit beeps to signify it has preheated, place the skewers on the Grill Grate. Close the hood and GRILL for 8 minutes without flipping.

5. After 8 minutes, check the steak for desired doneness, grilling up to 4 minutes more if desired.

6. When cooking is complete, serve immediately.

Ranch And Cheddar Pork Chops

Servings: 6
Cooking Time: 10 Minutes
Ingredients:

- 8 ounces cream cheese, at room temperature
- 1 tablespoon ranch seasoning mix
- ½ cup shredded cheddar cheese
- 6 (6-ounce) boneless pork chops

Directions:

1. Insert the Grill Grate and close the hood. Select GRILL, set the temperature to HI, and set the time to 10 minutes. Select START/STOP to begin preheating.

2. While the unit is preheating, in a small bowl, combine the cream cheese, ranch seasoning, and cheddar cheese.

3. When the unit beeps to signify it has preheated, place the pork chops on the Grill Grate. Close the hood and grill for 5 minutes.

4. After 5 minutes, open the hood and flip the chops. Then top each with the ranch-cheese mixture. Close the hood and cook for 5 minutes more.

5. When cooking is complete, remove the chops from the grill and serve.

Beef And Scallion Rolls

Servings: 4

Cooking Time: 10 Minutes

Ingredients:

- 1 pound skirt steak, very thinly sliced (12 slices)
- Salt
- Freshly ground black pepper
- 6 scallions, both white and green parts, halved lengthwise
- 2 tablespoons cornstarch
- ¼ cup water
- ¼ cup soy sauce
- 2 tablespoons light brown sugar, packed
- 1 teaspoon peeled minced fresh ginger
- 1 teaspoon garlic powder

Directions:

1. Insert the Grill Grate and close the hood. Select GRILL, set the temperature to HI, and set the time to 10 minutes. Select START/STOP to begin preheating.

2. While the unit is preheating, season each steak slice with salt and pepper. With one of the longer sides of a steak slice closest to you, place a scallion length at the bottom, and roll away from you to wrap the scallion. Sprinkle cornstarch on the outer layer of the rolled-up steak. Repeat for the remaining steak slices, scallions, and cornstarch.

3. In a small bowl, mix together the water, soy sauce, brown sugar, ginger, and garlic until the sugar is dissolved.

4. When the unit beeps to signify it has preheated, dip each beef roll in the soy sauce mixture and place it on the Grill Grate, seam-side down. Close the hood and grill for 5 minutes.

5. After 5 minutes, open the hood and flip the beef rolls. Brush each roll with the marinade. Close the hood and cook for 5 minutes more.

6. When cooking is complete, remove the beef rolls from the grill and serve.

Tonkatsu

Servings: 4

Cooking Time: 10 Minutes Per Batch

Ingredients:

- ⅔ cup all-purpose flour
- 2 large egg whites
- 1 cup panko breadcrumbs
- 4 center-cut boneless pork loin chops (about ½ inch thick)
- Cooking spray

Directions:

1. Spritz the Crisper Basket with cooking spray.

2. Insert the Crisper Basket and close the hood. Select AIR CRISP, set the temperature to 375°F, and set the time to 10 minutes. Select START/STOP to begin preheating.

3. Pour the flour in a bowl. Whisk the egg whites in a separate bowl. Spread the breadcrumbs on a large plate.

4. Dredge the pork loin chops in the flour first, press to coat well, then shake the excess off and dunk the chops in the eggs whites, and then roll the chops over the breadcrumbs. Shake the excess off.

5. Arrange the pork chops in batches in a single layer in the basket and spritz with cooking spray.

6. Close the hood and AIR CRISP for 10 minutes or until the pork chops are lightly browned and crunchy. Flip the chops halfway through. Repeat with remaining chops.

7. Serve immediately.

Garlic Herb Crusted Lamb

Servings: 6
Cooking Time: 1 Hour
Ingredients:
- ¼ cup red wine vinegar
- 3 garlic cloves, minced
- 1 tablespoon garlic powder
- 1 tablespoon paprika
- 1 tablespoon ground cumin
- 1 tablespoon dried parsley
- 1 tablespoon dried thyme
- 1 tablespoon dried oregano
- 1 teaspoon salt
- ½ teaspoon freshly ground black pepper
- Juice of ½ lemon
- 1 (3-pound) boneless leg of lamb

Directions:
1. In a large bowl, mix together the vinegar, garlic, garlic powder, paprika, cumin, parsley, thyme, oregano, salt, pepper, and lemon juice until well combined—the marinade will turn into a thick paste. Add the leg of lamb and massage the marinade into the meat. Coat the lamb with the marinade and let sit for at least 30 minutes. If marinating for longer, cover and refrigerate.
2. Plug the thermometer into the unit. Insert the Grill Grate and close the hood. Select GRILL, set the temperature to LO, and set the time to 30 minutes. Insert the Smart Thermometer into the thickest part of the meat. Select START/STOP to begin preheating.
3. When the unit beeps to signify it has preheated, place the lamb on the Grill Grate. Select the BEEF/LAMB preset and choose MEDIUM-WELL or according to your desired doneness. Close the hood and cook for 30 minutes.
4. After 30 minutes, which is the maximum time for the LO setting, select GRILL again, set the temperature to LO, and set the time to 30 minutes. Select START/STOP and press PREHEAT to skip preheating. Cook until the Smart Thermometer indicates that the desired internal temperature has been reached.
5. When cooking is complete, remove the lamb from the grill and serve.

Spaghetti Squash Lasagna

Servings: 6
Cooking Time: 1 Hour 15 Minutes
Ingredients:
- 2 large spaghetti squash, cooked
- 4 pounds ground beef
- 1 large jar Marinara sauce
- 25 slices Mozzarella cheese
- 30 ounces whole-milk ricotta cheese

Directions:
1. Select BAKE, set the temperature to 375ºF, and set the time to 45 minutes. Select START/STOP to begin preheating.
2. Slice the spaghetti squash and place it face down inside a baking pan. Fill with water until covered.
3. Place the pan directly in the pot. Close the hood and BAKE for 45 minutes until skin is soft.
4. Sear the ground beef in a skillet over medium-high heat for 5 minutes or until browned, then add the marinara sauce and heat until warm. Set aside.
5. Scrape the flesh off the cooked squash to resemble strands of spaghetti.
6. Layer the lasagna in a large greased pan in alternating layers of spaghetti squash, beef sauce, Mozzarella, ricotta. Repeat until all the ingredients have been used.
7. Place the pan directly in the pot. Close the hood and BAKE for 30 minutes.
8. Serve.

Stuffed-onion Burgers

Servings: 6
Cooking Time: 15 Minutes
Ingredients:

- 2 large red onions
- 1 teaspoon onion powder
- 1 teaspoon garlic powder
- 2 teaspoons sea salt
- 2 teaspoons freshly ground black pepper
- 4 tablespoons gluten-free Worcestershire sauce
- 2 pounds ground beef

Directions:

1. Cut both ends off the onions. Slice each onion crosswise into thirds and peel off the papery outer skin. Separate the outer two rings (keeping the pair together) from each third for a stable and firm onion ring wrapper.
2. Insert the Grill Grate and close the hood. Select GRILL, set the temperature to HI, and set the time to 15 minutes. Select START/STOP to begin preheating.
3. In a large bowl, combine the onion powder, garlic powder, salt, pepper, and Worcestershire sauce. Add the ground beef in chunks and loosely mix. Form the mixture into 6 equal-size patties. Stuff the burger patties into the onion rings and make a small indentation in the middle of each patty with your thumb.
4. When the unit beeps to signify it has preheated, place the patties on the Grill Grate. Close the hood and grill for 7 minutes, 30 seconds.
5. After 7 minutes, 30 seconds, open the hood and flip the burgers. Close the hood and cook for 7 minutes, 30 seconds more for medium-well burgers. If you prefer your burgers more well-done, continue cooking to your liking.
6. When cooking is complete, remove the burgers from the grill and serve.

Korean-style Steak Tips

Servings: 4
Cooking Time: 13 Minutes
Ingredients:

- 4 garlic cloves, minced
- ½ apple, peeled and grated
- 3 tablespoons sesame oil
- 3 tablespoons brown sugar
- ⅓ cup soy sauce
- 1 teaspoon freshly ground black pepper
- Sea salt
- 1½ pounds beef tips

Directions:

1. In a medium bowl, combine the garlic, apple, sesame oil, sugar, soy sauce, pepper, and salt until well mixed.
2. Place the beef tips in a large shallow bowl and pour the marinade over them. Cover and refrigerate for 30 minutes.
3. Insert the Grill Grate and close the hood. Select GRILL, set the temperature to MEDIUM, and set the time to 13 minutes. Select START/STOP to begin preheating.
4. When the unit beeps to signify it has preheated, place the steak tips on the Grill Grate. Close the hood and GRILL for 11 minutes.
5. Cooking is complete to medium doneness when the internal temperature of the meat reaches 145°F on a food thermometer. If desired, GRILL for up to 2 minutes more.
6. Remove the steak, and set it on a cutting board to rest for 5 minutes. Serve.

Pork Sausage With Cauliflower Mash

Servings: 6
Cooking Time: 27 Minutes
Ingredients:

- 1 pound cauliflower, chopped
- 6 pork sausages, chopped
- ½ onion, sliced
- 3 eggs, beaten
- ⅓ cup Colby cheese
- 1 teaspoon cumin powder
- ½ teaspoon tarragon
- ½ teaspoon sea salt
- ½ teaspoon ground black pepper
- Cooking spray

Directions:

1. Select BAKE, set the temperature to 365°F, and set the time to 27 minutes. Select START/STOP to begin preheating.
2. Spritz a baking pan with cooking spray.
3. In a saucepan over medium heat, boil the cauliflower until tender. Place the boiled cauliflower in a food processor and pulse until puréed. Transfer to a large bowl and combine with remaining ingredients until well blended.
4. Pour the cauliflower and sausage mixture into the baking pan. Place the pan directly in the pot. Close the hood and BAKE for 27 minutes, or until lightly browned.
5. Divide the mixture among six serving dishes and serve warm.

Meatless Recipes

Cinnamon-spiced Acorn Squash

Servings: 2
Cooking Time: 15 Minutes
Ingredients:

- 1 medium acorn squash, halved crosswise and deseeded
- 1 teaspoon coconut oil
- 1 teaspoon light brown sugar
- Few dashes of ground cinnamon
- Few dashes of ground nutmeg

Directions:

1. Insert the Crisper Basket and close the hood. Select AIR CRISP, set the temperature to 325°F, and set the time to 15 minutes. Select START/STOP to begin preheating.
2. On a clean work surface, rub the cut sides of the acorn squash with coconut oil. Scatter with the brown sugar, cinnamon, and nutmeg.
3. Put the squash halves in the Crisper Basket, cut-side up. Close the hood and AIR CRISP for 15 minutes until just tender when pierced in the center with a paring knife.
4. Rest for 5 to 10 minutes and serve warm.

Flatbread Pizza

Servings: 4
Cooking Time: 10 Minutes
Ingredients:
- 1 (14-ounce) package refrigerated pizza dough
- 2 tablespoons extra-virgin olive oil
- ½ cup prepared Alfredo sauce
- 1 medium zucchini, cut into ⅛-inch-thick discs
- ½ cup fresh spinach
- ½ red onion, sliced
- 4 cherry tomatoes, sliced

Directions:
1. Insert the Grill Grate and close the hood. Select GRILL, set the temperature to MED, and set the time to 10 minutes. Select START/STOP to begin preheating.
2. While the unit is preheating, roll out the dough into a rectangle slightly smaller than the Grill Grate (8 by 11 inches). Brush the olive oil on both sides of the dough.
3. When the unit beeps to signify it has preheated, place the dough on the Grill Grate. Close the hood and grill for 5 minutes.
4. After 5 minutes, open the hood and flip the dough. (Or skip flipping, if you'd rather.) Spread the Alfredo sauce across the dough, leaving a 1-inch border. Layer the zucchini, spinach, red onion, and cherry tomatoes across the dough. Close the hood and cook for 5 minutes more.
5. When cooking is complete, remove the pizza from the grill. Slice and serve.

Crusted Brussels Sprouts With Sage

Servings: 4
Cooking Time: 15 Minutes
Ingredients:
- 1 pound Brussels sprouts, halved
- 1 cup bread crumbs
- 2 tablespoons grated Grana Padano cheese
- 1 tablespoon paprika
- 2 tablespoons canola oil
- 1 tablespoon chopped sage

Directions:
1. Line the Crisper Basket with parchment paper.
2. Insert the Crisper Basket and close the hood. Select ROAST, set the temperature to 400°F, and set the time to 15 minutes. Select START/STOP to begin preheating.
3. In a small bowl, thoroughly mix the bread crumbs, cheese, and paprika. In a large bowl, place the Brussels sprouts and drizzle the canola oil over the top. Sprinkle with the bread crumb mixture and toss to coat.
4. Place the Brussels sprouts in the Crisper Basket. Close the hood and ROAST for 15 minutes, or until the Brussels sprouts are lightly browned and crisp. Shake the basket a few times during cooking to ensure even cooking.
5. Transfer the Brussels sprouts to a plate and sprinkle the sage on top before serving.

Charred Green Beans With Sesame Seeds

Servings: 4
Cooking Time: 8 Minutes
Ingredients:

- 1 tablespoon reduced-sodium soy sauce or tamari
- ½ tablespoon Sriracha sauce
- 4 teaspoons toasted sesame oil, divided
- 12 ounces trimmed green beans
- ½ tablespoon toasted sesame seeds

Directions:

1. Insert the Crisper Basket and close the hood. Select AIR CRISP, set the temperature to 375ºF, and set the time to 8 minutes. Select START/STOP to begin preheating.
2. Whisk together the soy sauce, Sriracha sauce, and 1 teaspoon of sesame oil in a small bowl until smooth.
3. Toss the green beans with the remaining sesame oil in a large bowl until evenly coated.
4. Place the green beans in the Crisper Basket in a single layer. You may need to work in batches to avoid overcrowding.
5. Close the hood and AIR CRISP for 8 minutes until the green beans are lightly charred and tender. Shake the basket halfway through the cooking time.
6. Remove from the basket to a platter. Repeat with the remaining green beans.
7. Pour the prepared sauce over the top of green beans and toss well. Serve sprinkled with the toasted sesame seeds.

Cheese And Spinach Stuffed Portobellos

Servings: 4
Cooking Time: 8 Minutes
Ingredients:

- 4 large portobello mushrooms, rinsed, stemmed, and gills removed
- 4 ounces cream cheese, at room temperature
- ½ cup mayonnaise
- ½ cup sour cream
- 1 teaspoon onion powder
- ¼ teaspoon garlic powder
- ¼ cup grated Parmesan cheese
- ½ cup shredded mozzarella cheese
- 2 cups fresh spinach

Directions:

1. Insert the Grill Grate and close the hood. Select GRILL, set the temperature to HI, and set the time to 8 minutes. Select START/STOP to begin preheating.
2. When the unit beeps to signify it has preheated, place the mushrooms on the Grill Grate, cap-side up. Close the hood and cook for 4 minutes.
3. While the mushrooms are grilling, in a large bowl, combine the cream cheese, mayonnaise, sour cream, onion powder, garlic powder, Parmesan cheese, mozzarella cheese, and spinach. Mix well.
4. After 4 minutes, open the hood and flip the mushrooms. Evenly distribute the filling inside the caps. Close the hood and cook for 4 minutes more.
5. When cooking is complete, remove the stuffed mushrooms from the grill and serve.

Vegetable And Cheese Stuffed Tomatoes

Servings: 4
Cooking Time: 16 To 20 Minutes
Ingredients:

- 4 medium beefsteak tomatoes, rinsed
- ½ cup grated carrot
- 1 medium onion, chopped
- 1 garlic clove, minced
- 2 teaspoons olive oil
- 2 cups fresh baby spinach
- ¼ cup crumbled low-sodium feta cheese
- ½ teaspoon dried basil

Directions:

1. Select BAKE, set the temperature to 350°F, and set the time to 20 minutes. Select START/STOP to begin preheating.
2. On your cutting board, cut a thin slice off the top of each tomato. Scoop out a ¼- to ½-inch-thick tomato pulp and place the tomatoes upside down on paper towels to drain. Set aside.
3. Stir together the carrot, onion, garlic, and olive oil in a baking pan. Place the pan directly in the pot. Close the hood and BAKE for 4 to 6 minutes, or until the carrot is crisp-tender.
4. Remove the pan from the grill and stir in the spinach, feta cheese, and basil.
5. Spoon ¼ of the vegetable mixture into each tomato and transfer the stuffed tomatoes to the pan.
6. Place the pan directly in the pot. Close the hood and BAKE for 12 to 14 minutes, or until the filling is hot and the tomatoes are lightly caramelized.
7. Let the tomatoes cool for 5 minutes and serve.

Green Beans With Sun-dried Tomatoes And Feta

Servings: 8
Cooking Time: 8 Minutes
Ingredients:

- 2 pounds green beans, ends trimmed
- 2 tablespoons extra-virgin olive oil
- 1 teaspoon salt
- ½ teaspoon freshly ground black pepper
- 1 cup sun-dried tomatoes packed in oil, undrained, sliced
- 6 ounces feta cheese, crumbled

Directions:

1. Insert the Grill Grate and close the hood. Select GRILL, set the temperature to HI, and set the time to 8 minutes. Select START/STOP to begin preheating.
2. While the unit is preheating, in a large bowl, toss the green beans with the olive oil, salt, and pepper.
3. When the unit beeps to signify it has preheated, place the green beans on the Grill Grate. Close the hood and grill for 4 minutes.
4. After 4 minutes, open the hood and flip the green beans. Close the hood and cook for 4 minutes more.
5. When cooking is complete, transfer the green beans to a large bowl. Add the sun-dried tomatoes and mix together. Top with the feta cheese and serve.

Arugula And Broccoli Salad

Servings: 4
Cooking Time: 12 Minutes

Ingredients:

- 2 heads broccoli, trimmed into florets
- ½ red onion, sliced
- 1 tablespoon canola oil
- 2 tablespoons extra-virgin olive oil
- 1 tablespoon freshly squeezed lemon juice
- 1 teaspoon honey
- 1 teaspoon Dijon mustard
- 1 garlic clove, minced
- Pinch red pepper flakes
- ¼ teaspoon fine sea salt
- Freshly ground black pepper, to taste
- 4 cups arugula, torn
- 2 tablespoons grated Parmesan cheese

Directions:

1. Insert the Grill Grate and close the hood. Select GRILL, set the temperature to MAX, and set the time to 12 minutes. Select START/STOP to begin preheating.
2. While the unit is preheating, in a large bowl, combine the broccoli, sliced onions, and canola oil and toss until coated.
3. When the unit beeps to signify it has preheated, place the vegetables on the Grill Grate. Close the hood and GRILL for 8 to 12 minutes, until charred on all sides.
4. Meanwhile, in a medium bowl, whisk together the olive oil, lemon juice, honey, mustard, garlic, red pepper flakes, salt, and pepper.
5. When cooking is complete, combine the roasted vegetables and arugula in a large serving bowl. Drizzle with the vinaigrette, and sprinkle with the Parmesan cheese.

Potatoes With Zucchinis

Servings: 4
Cooking Time: 45 Minutes

Ingredients:

- 2 potatoes, peeled and cubed
- 4 carrots, cut into chunks
- 1 head broccoli, cut into florets
- 4 zucchinis, sliced thickly
- Salt and ground black pepper, to taste
- ¼ cup olive oil
- 1 tablespoon dry onion powder

Directions:

1. Select BAKE, set the temperature to 400°F, and set the time to 45 minutes. Select START/STOP to begin preheating.
2. In a baking pan, add all the ingredients and combine well.
3. Place the pan directly in the pot. Close the hood and BAKE for 45 minutes, ensuring the vegetables are soft and the sides have browned before serving.

Grilled Artichokes With Garlic Aioli

Servings: 4

Cooking Time: 33 Minutes

Ingredients:

- For the artichokes
- 4 artichokes
- 8 tablespoons avocado oil
- 8 tablespoons minced garlic
- Salt
- Freshly ground black pepper
- For the garlic aioli
- ½ cup mayonnaise
- 1 garlic clove, minced
- 1 tablespoon apple cider vinegar
- ⅛ teaspoon paprika

Directions:

1. Pull off the tough outer leaves near the stem of the artichoke and trim the bottom of the stem. Cut off the top third (½ to 1 inch) of the artichoke. Trim the tips of the leaves that surround the artichoke, as they can be sharp and thorny. Then cut the artichoke in half lengthwise. This exposes the artichoke heart. Use a spoon to remove the fuzzy choke, scraping to make sure it is cleaned away, then rinse the artichoke.

2. Insert the Grill Grate and close the hood. Select GRILL, set the temperature to LO, and set the time to 25 minutes. Select START/STOP to begin preheating.

3. While the unit is preheating, prepare 8 large pieces of aluminum foil for wrapping. Place an artichoke half, cut-side up, in the center of a foil piece. Drizzle 1 tablespoon of avocado oil into the center of the artichoke half and add 1 tablespoon of minced garlic. Season with salt and pepper. Seal the foil packet, making sure all sides are closed. Repeat for each artichoke half.

4. When the unit beeps to signify it has preheated, place the foil-wrapped artichokes on the Grill Grate. Close the hood and grill for 25 minutes.

5. When cooking is complete, the stem and heart will be soft, about the consistency of a cooked potato. Remove the artichokes from the foil.

6. Select GRILL, set the temperature to MAX, and set the time to 8 minutes. Place the artichokes on the Grill Grate, cut-side down. Select START/STOP and then press the PREHEAT button to skip preheating. Close the hood and cook for 4 minutes.

7. After 4 minutes, open the hood and flip the artichokes. Season with additional salt and pepper, if desired. Close the hood and cook for 4 minutes more.

8. When cooking is complete, remove the artichokes from the grill.

9. In a small bowl, combine the mayonnaise, garlic, vinegar, and paprika. Serve alongside the artichokes for dipping.

Zucchini And Onions Au Gratin

Servings: 4
Cooking Time: 15 Minutes

Ingredients:

- 1 cup panko bread crumbs
- 1 cup grated Parmesan cheese
- 1 large white onion, sliced
- 3 zucchini, cut into thin discs
- 1 teaspoon sea salt
- 1 teaspoon freshly ground black pepper
- 1 teaspoon onion powder
- 1 cup heavy (whipping) cream
- 1 tablespoon unsalted butter, at room temperature
- 1 teaspoon cornstarch

Directions:

1. Insert the Cooking Pot and close the hood. Select GRILL, set the temperature to MED, and set the time to 15 minutes. Select START/STOP to begin preheating.

2. While the unit is preheating, in a large bowl, combine the panko bread crumbs and Parmesan cheese.

3. When the unit beeps to signify it has preheated, add the onion to the Cooking Pot. Close the hood and cook for 2 minutes.

4. After 2 minutes, open the hood and add the zucchini, salt, pepper, and onion powder. Stir to mix. Close the hood and cook for 2 minutes.

5. After 2 minutes, open the hood and stir in the heavy cream, butter, and cornstarch. Close the hood and cook for 3 minutes.

6. After 3 minutes, the vegetable mixture should be creamy and thick. Evenly spread the bread crumb mixture over the top. Close the hood and cook for 8 minutes more.

7. When cooking is complete, the top will be golden brown and crunchy. Remove from the grill and serve.

Sriracha Golden Cauliflower

Servings: 4
Cooking Time: 17 Minutes

Ingredients:

- ¼ cup vegan butter, melted
- ¼ cup sriracha sauce
- 4 cups cauliflower florets
- 1 cup bread crumbs
- 1 teaspoon salt

Directions:

1. Insert the Crisper Basket and close the hood. Select AIR CRISP, set the temperature to 375°F, and set the time to 17 minutes. Select START/STOP to begin preheating.

2. Mix the sriracha and vegan butter in a bowl and pour this mixture over the cauliflower, taking care to cover each floret entirely.

3. In a separate bowl, combine the bread crumbs and salt.

4. Dip the cauliflower florets in the bread crumbs, coating each one well. Transfer to the basket. Close the hood and AIR CRISP for 17 minutes.

5. Serve hot.

Chermoula Beet Roast

Servings: 4
Cooking Time: 25 Minutes
Ingredients:

- Chermoula:
- 1 cup packed fresh cilantro leaves
- ½ cup packed fresh parsley leaves
- 6 cloves garlic, peeled
- 2 teaspoons smoked paprika
- 2 teaspoons ground cumin
- 1 teaspoon ground coriander
- ½ to 1 teaspoon cayenne pepper
- Pinch of crushed saffron (optional)
- ½ cup extra-virgin olive oil
- Kosher salt, to taste
- Beets:
- 3 medium beets, trimmed, peeled, and cut into 1-inch chunks
- 2 tablespoons chopped fresh cilantro
- 2 tablespoons chopped fresh parsley

Directions:

1. In a food processor, combine the cilantro, parsley, garlic, paprika, cumin, coriander, and cayenne. Pulse until coarsely chopped. Add the saffron, if using, and process until combined. With the food processor running, slowly add the olive oil in a steady stream; process until the sauce is uniform. Season with salt.
2. Insert the Crisper Basket and close the hood. Select ROAST, set the temperature to 375ºF, and set the time to 25 minutes. Select START/STOP to begin preheating.
3. In a large bowl, drizzle the beets with ½ cup of the chermoula to coat. Arrange the beets in the Crisper Basket. Close the hood and ROAST for 25 minutes, or until the beets are tender.
4. Transfer the beets to a serving platter. Sprinkle with the chopped cilantro and parsley and serve.

Loaded Zucchini Boats

Servings: 4
Cooking Time: 10 Minutes
Ingredients:

- 4 medium zucchini
- 1 cup panko bread crumbs
- 2 garlic cloves, minced
- ½ small white onion, diced
- ½ cup grated Parmesan cheese
- 1 tablespoon Italian seasoning

Directions:

1. Insert the Grill Grate and close the hood. Select GRILL, set the temperature to HI, and set the time to 10 minutes. Select START/STOP to begin preheating.
2. While the unit is preheating, cut the zucchini in half lengthwise. Carefully scoop out the flesh and put it in a medium bowl. Set the boats aside.
3. Add the panko bread crumbs, garlic, onion, Parmesan cheese, and Italian seasoning to the bowl and mix well. Spoon the filling into each zucchini half.
4. When the unit beeps to signify it has preheated, place the zucchini boats on the Grill Grate, cut-side up. Close the hood and grill for 10 minutes.
5. When cooking is complete, the cheese will be melted and the tops will be crispy and golden brown. Remove the zucchini boats from the grill and serve.

Simple Ratatouille

Servings: 2
Cooking Time: 16 Minutes
Ingredients:

- 2 Roma tomatoes, thinly sliced
- 1 zucchini, thinly sliced
- 2 yellow bell peppers, sliced
- 2 garlic cloves, minced
- 2 tablespoons olive oil
- 2 tablespoons herbes de Provence
- 1 tablespoon vinegar
- Salt and black pepper, to taste

Directions:

1. Select ROAST, set the temperature to 390°F, and set the time to 16 minutes. Select START/STOP to begin preheating.
2. Place the tomatoes, zucchini, bell peppers, garlic, olive oil, herbes de Provence, and vinegar in a large bowl and toss until the vegetables are evenly coated. Sprinkle with salt and pepper and toss again. Pour the vegetable mixture into the pot.
3. Close the hood and ROAST for 8 minutes. Stir and continue roasting for 8 minutes until tender.
4. Let the vegetable mixture stand for 5 minutes in the basket before removing and serving.

Black Bean And Tomato Chili

Servings: 6
Cooking Time: 23 Minutes
Ingredients:

- 1 tablespoon olive oil
- 1 medium onion, diced
- 3 garlic cloves, minced
- 1 cup vegetable broth
- 3 cans black beans, drained and rinsed
- 2 cans diced tomatoes
- 2 chipotle peppers, chopped
- 2 teaspoons cumin
- 2 teaspoons chili powder
- 1 teaspoon dried oregano
- ½ teaspoon salt

Directions:

1. Over a medium heat, fry the garlic and onions in the olive oil for 3 minutes.
2. Add the remaining ingredients, stirring constantly and scraping the bottom to prevent sticking.
3. Select BAKE, set the temperature to 400°F, and set the time to 20 minutes. Select START/STOP to begin preheating.
4. Take a baking pan and place the mixture inside. Put a sheet of aluminum foil on top.
5. Place the pan directly in the pot. Close the hood and BAKE for 20 minutes.
6. When ready, plate up and serve immediately.

Asian-inspired Broccoli

Servings: 2
Cooking Time: 10 Minutes
Ingredients:

- 12 ounces broccoli florets
- 2 tablespoons Asian hot chili oil
- 1 teaspoon ground Sichuan peppercorns (or black pepper)
- 2 garlic cloves, finely chopped
- 1 piece fresh ginger, peeled and finely chopped
- Kosher salt and freshly ground black pepper

Directions:

1. Insert the Crisper Basket and close the hood. Select ROAST, set the temperature to 375ºF, and set the time to 10 minutes. Select START/STOP to begin preheating.
2. Toss the broccoli florets with the chili oil, Sichuan peppercorns, garlic, ginger, salt, and pepper in a mixing bowl until thoroughly coated.
3. Transfer the broccoli florets to the Crisper Basket. Close the hood and ROAST for 10 minutes, shaking the basket halfway through, or until the broccoli florets are lightly browned and tender.
4. Remove the broccoli from the basket and serve on a plate.

Double "egg" Plant (eggplant Omelets)

Servings: 4
Cooking Time: 16 Minutes
Ingredients:

- 4 Chinese eggplants
- 2 large eggs
- Garlic powder
- Salt
- Freshly ground black pepper
- ¼ cup ketchup
- 1 tablespoon hot sauce (optional)

Directions:

1. Insert the Grill Grate. Select GRILL, set the temperature to HI, and set the time to 10 minutes. Select START/STOP to begin preheating.
2. When the unit beeps to signify it has preheated, place the whole eggplants on the Grill Grate. Close the hood and cook for 5 minutes.
3. After 5 minutes, open the hood and flip the eggplants. Close the hood and cook for 5 minutes more.
4. When cooking is complete, the eggplant skin will be charred and cracked and the flesh will be soft. Remove the eggplants from the grill and set aside to cool.
5. Once the eggplants have cooled down, peel the skin. Then, using a fork, flatten the eggplants with a brushing motion until they become pear shaped and about the thickness of a pancake.
6. Select GRILL, set the temperature to HI, and set the time to 6 minutes. Select START/STOP to begin preheating.
7. While the unit is preheating, in a large bowl, whisk the eggs. Dip each eggplant into the egg mixture to coat both sides, then season both sides with garlic powder, salt, and pepper.
8. When the grill beeps to signify it has preheated, place the coated eggplants on the Grill Grate. Close the hood and grill for 3 minutes.
9. After 3 minutes, open the hood and flip the eggplants. Close the hood and cook for 3 minutes more. Add more time if needed until you get your desired crispiness of the omelets.
10. When cooking is complete, remove the eggplant omelets from the grill. In a small bowl, combine the ketchup and hot sauce (if using), or just use ketchup if you do not like spice, and serve alongside the omelets for dipping.

Veggie Taco Pie

Servings: 4

Cooking Time: 15 Minutes

Ingredients:

- 1 (15-ounce) can pinto beans, drained and rinsed
- 1 tablespoon chili powder
- 2 teaspoons ground cumin
- 2 teaspoons sea salt
- 1 teaspoon paprika
- ½ teaspoon garlic powder
- ½ teaspoon onion powder
- ½ teaspoon dried oregano
- 4 small flour tortillas
- 1 cup sour cream
- 1 (14-ounce) can diced tomatoes, drained
- 1 (15-ounce) can black beans, drained and rinsed
- 2 cups shredded cheddar cheese

Directions:

1. Insert the Cooking Pot and close the hood. Select BAKE, set the temperature to 350°F, and set the time to 15 minutes. Select START/STOP to begin preheating.

2. While the unit is preheating, in a large bowl, mash the pinto beans with a fork. Add the chili powder, cumin, salt, paprika, garlic powder, onion powder, and oregano and mix until well combined. Place a tortilla in the bottom of a 6-inch springform pan. Spread a quarter of the mashed pinto beans on the tortilla in an even layer, then layer on a quarter each of the sour cream, tomatoes, black beans, and cheddar cheese in that order. Repeat the layers three more times, ending with cheese.

3. When the unit beeps to signify it has preheated, place the pan in the Cooking Pot. Close the hood and cook for 15 minutes.

4. When cooking is complete, the cheese will be melted. Remove the pan from the grill and serve.

Perfect Grilled Asparagus

Servings: 4

Cooking Time: 6 Minutes

Ingredients:

- 24 asparagus spears, woody ends trimmed
- Extra-virgin olive oil, for drizzling
- Sea salt
- Freshly ground black pepper

Directions:

1. Insert the Grill Grate and close the hood. Select GRILL, set the temperature to HI, and set the time to 6 minutes. Select START/STOP to begin preheating.

2. While the unit is preheating, place the asparagus in a large bowl and drizzle with the olive oil. Toss to coat, then season with salt and pepper.

3. When the unit beeps to signify it has preheated, place the spears evenly spread out on the Grill Grate. Close the hood and grill for 3 minutes.

4. After 3 minutes, open the hood and flip and move the spears around. Close the hood and cook for 3 minutes more.

5. When cooking is complete, remove the asparagus from the grill and serve.

Tofu, Carrot And Cauliflower Rice

Servings: 4
Cooking Time: 22 Minutes
Ingredients:

- ½ block tofu, crumbled
- 1 cup diced carrot
- ½ cup diced onions
- 2 tablespoons soy sauce
- 1 teaspoon turmeric
- Cauliflower:
- 3 cups cauliflower rice
- ½ cup chopped broccoli
- ½ cup frozen peas
- 2 tablespoons soy sauce
- 1 tablespoon minced ginger
- 2 garlic cloves, minced
- 1 tablespoon rice vinegar
- 1½ teaspoons toasted sesame oil

Directions:

1. Select ROAST, set the temperature to 370°F, and set the time to 22 minutes. Select START/STOP to begin preheating.
2. Mix together the tofu, carrot, onions, soy sauce, and turmeric in the pot and stir until well incorporated.
3. Place the pot in the grill. Close the hood and ROAST for 10 minutes.
4. Meanwhile, in a large bowl, combine all the ingredients for the cauliflower and toss well.
5. Remove the pot and add the cauliflower mixture to the tofu and stir to combine.
6. Return the pot to the grill and continue roasting for 12 minutes, or until the vegetables are cooked to your preference.
7. Cool for 5 minutes before serving.

Balsamic Mushroom Sliders With Pesto

Servings: 4
Cooking Time: 8 Minutes
Ingredients:

- 8 small portobello mushrooms, trimmed with gills removed
- 2 tablespoons canola oil
- 2 tablespoons balsamic vinegar
- 8 slider buns
- 1 tomato, sliced
- ½ cup pesto
- ½ cup micro greens

Directions:

1. Insert the Grill Grate and close the hood. Select GRILL, set the temperature to HIGH, and set the time to 8 minutes. Select START/STOP to begin preheating.
2. While the unit is preheating, brush the mushrooms with the oil and balsamic vinegar.
3. When the unit beeps to signify it has preheated, place the mushrooms, gill-side down, on the Grill Grate. Close the hood and GRILL for 8 minutes until the mushrooms are tender.
4. When cooking is complete, remove the mushrooms from the grill, and layer on the buns with tomato, pesto, and micro greens.

Summer Squash And Zucchini Salad

Servings: 4
Cooking Time: 20 Minutes
Ingredients:

- 1 zucchini, sliced lengthwise about ¼-inch thick
- 1 summer squash, sliced lengthwise about ¼-inch thick
- ½ red onion, sliced
- 4 tablespoons canola oil, divided
- 2 portobello mushroom caps, trimmed with gills removed
- 2 ears corn, shucked
- 2 teaspoons freshly squeezed lemon juice
- Sea salt, to taste
- Freshly ground black pepper, to taste

Directions:

1. Insert the Grill Grate and close the hood. Select GRILL, set the temperature to MAX, and set the time to 25 minutes. Select START/STOP to begin preheating.
2. Meanwhile, in a large bowl, toss the zucchini, squash, and onion with 2 tablespoons of oil until evenly coated.
3. When the unit beeps to signify it has preheated, arrange the zucchini, squash, and onions on the Grill Grate. Close the hood and GRILL for 6 minutes.
4. After 6 minutes, open the hood and flip the squash. Close the hood and GRILL for 6 to 9 minutes more.
5. Meanwhile, brush the mushrooms and corn with the remaining 2 tablespoons of oil.
6. When cooking is complete, remove the zucchini, squash, and onions and swap in the mushrooms and corn. Close the hood and GRILL for the remaining 10 minutes.
7. When cooking is complete, remove the mushrooms and corn, and let cool.
8. Cut the kernels from the cobs. Roughly chop all the vegetables into bite-size pieces.
9. Place the vegetables in a serving bowl and drizzle with lemon juice. Season with salt and pepper, and toss until evenly mixed.

Cheesy Macaroni Balls

Servings: 2
Cooking Time: 10 Minutes
Ingredients:

- 2 cups leftover macaroni
- 1 cup shredded Cheddar cheese
- ½ cup flour
- 1 cup bread crumbs
- 3 large eggs
- 1 cup milk
- ½ teaspoon salt
- ¼ teaspoon black pepper

Directions:

1. Insert the Crisper Basket and close the hood. Select AIR CRISP, set the temperature to 365°F, and set the time to 10 minutes. Select START/STOP to begin preheating.
2. In a bowl, combine the leftover macaroni and shredded cheese.
3. Pour the flour in a separate bowl. Put the bread crumbs in a third bowl. Finally, in a fourth bowl, mix the eggs and milk with a whisk.
4. With an ice-cream scoop, create balls from the macaroni mixture. Coat them the flour, then in the egg mixture, and lastly in the bread crumbs.
5. Arrange the balls in the basket. Close the hood and AIR CRISP for 10 minutes, giving them an occasional stir. Ensure they crisp up nicely.
6. Serve hot.

Bean And Corn Stuffed Peppers

Servings: 6
Cooking Time: 32 Minutes
Ingredients:

- 6 red or green bell peppers, seeded, ribs removed, and top ½-inch cut off and reserved
- 4 garlic cloves, minced
- 1 small white onion, diced
- 2 bags instant rice, cooked in microwave
- 1 can red or green enchilada sauce
- ½ teaspoon chili powder
- ¼ teaspoon ground cumin
- ½ cup canned black beans, rinsed and drained
- ½ cup frozen corn
- ½ cup vegetable stock
- 1 bag shredded Colby Jack cheese, divided

Directions:

1. Chop the ½-inch portions of reserved bell pepper and place in a large mixing bowl. Add the garlic, onion, cooked instant rice, enchilada sauce, chili powder, cumin, black beans, corn, vegetable stock, and half the cheese. Mix to combine.
2. Use the cooking pot without the Grill Grate or Crisper Basket installed. Close the hood. Select ROAST, set the temperature to 350°F, and set the time to 32 minutes. Select START/STOP to begin preheating.
3. While the unit is preheating, spoon the mixture into the peppers, filling them up as full as possible. If necessary, lightly press the mixture down into the peppers to fit more in.
4. When the unit beeps to signify it has preheated, place the peppers, upright, in the pot. Close the hood and ROAST for 30 minutes.
5. After 30 minutes, sprinkle the remaining cheese over the top of the peppers. Close the hood and ROAST for the remaining 2 minutes.
6. When cooking is complete, serve immediately.

Grilled Vegetable Quesadillas

Servings: 4
Cooking Time: 8 Minutes
Ingredients:

- 1 medium onion, chopped
- 1 medium summer squash, halved lengthwise and thinly sliced into half-moons
- 1 medium zucchini, halved lengthwise and thinly sliced into half-moons
- Extra-virgin olive oil
- 4 (10-inch) flour tortillas
- 1 cup shredded mozzarella cheese
- ¼ cup chopped fresh cilantro (optional)

Directions:

1. Insert the Grill Grate and close the hood. Select GRILL, set the temperature to HI, and set the time to 8 minutes. Select START/STOP to begin preheating.
2. In a large bowl, combine the onion, summer squash, and zucchini and lightly coat with olive oil.
3. When the unit beeps to signify it has preheated, place the vegetables on the Grill Grate in a single layer. Close the hood and cook for 4 minutes.
4. While the vegetables are grilling, place the tortillas on a large tray and cover half of each with about ¼ cup of mozzarella.
5. After 4 minutes, open the hood and transfer the vegetables to the tortillas, evenly spreading on top of the cheese. Top the vegetables with the cilantro (if using). Fold the other half of each tortilla over to close. Place the quesadillas on the Grill Grate. Close the hood and cook for 2 minutes.
6. After 2 minutes, open the hood and flip the quesadillas. Close the hood and cook for 2 minutes more.
7. When cooking is complete, the cheese will be melted and the tortillas will be crispy. Remove the quesadillas from the grill and serve.

Sweet And Spicy Corn On The Cob

Servings: 6
Cooking Time: 12 Minutes
Ingredients:

- 6 ears corn, shucked
- Avocado oil, for drizzling
- Salt
- Freshly ground black pepper
- ½ cup sweet chili sauce
- ¼ cup sour cream
- ¼ cup mayonnaise
- 2 tablespoons sriracha
- Juice of 1 lime
- ¼ cup chopped cilantro, for garnish

Directions:

1. Insert the Grill Grate and close the hood. Select GRILL, set the temperature to MAX, and set the time to 12 minutes. Select START/STOP to begin preheating.
2. While the unit is preheating, drizzle the corn with avocado oil, rubbing it in to coat. Season with salt and pepper all over.
3. When the unit beeps to signify it has preheated, place the corn on the Grill Grate. Close the hood and grill for 6 minutes.
4. After 6 minutes, open the hood and flip the corn. Close the hood and cook 6 minutes more.
5. While the corn is cooking, in a small bowl, combine the sweet chili sauce, sour cream, mayonnaise, sriracha, and lime juice.
6. When cooking is complete, remove the corn from the grill. Coat the ears with the sweet chili sauce mixture. Garnish with the cilantro and serve.

Mozzarella Broccoli Calzones

Servings: 4
Cooking Time: 24 Minutes
Ingredients:

- 1 head broccoli, trimmed into florets
- 2 tablespoons extra-virgin olive oil
- 1 store-bought pizza dough
- 2 to 3 tablespoons all-purpose flour, plus more for dusting
- 1 egg, beaten
- 2 cups shredded Mozzarella cheese
- 1 cup ricotta cheese
- ½ cup grated Parmesan cheese
- 1 garlic clove, grated
- Grated zest of 1 lemon
- ½ teaspoon red pepper flakes
- Cooking oil spray

Directions:

1. Insert the Crisper Basket and close the hood. Select AIR CRISP, set the temperature to 390°F, and set the time to 12 minutes. Select START/STOP to begin preheating.
2. Meanwhile, in a large bowl, toss the broccoli and olive oil until evenly coated.

3. When the unit beeps to signify it has preheated, add the broccoli to the basket. Close the hood and AIR CRISP for 6 minutes.

4. While the broccoli is cooking, divide the pizza dough into four equal pieces. Dust a clean work surface with the flour. Place the dough on the floured surface and roll each piece into an 8-inch round of even thickness. Dust your rolling pin and work surface with additional flour, as needed, to ensure the dough does not stick. Brush a thin coating of egg wash around the edges of each round.

5. After 6 minutes, shake the basket of broccoli. Place the basket back in the unit and close the hood to resume cooking.

6. Meanwhile, in a medium bowl, combine the Mozzarella, ricotta, Parmesan cheese, garlic, lemon zest, and red pepper flakes.

7. After cooking is complete, add the broccoli to the cheese mixture. Spoon one-quarter of the mixture onto one side of each dough. Fold the other half over the filling, and press firmly to seal the edges together. Brush each calzone all over with the remaining egg wash.

8. Select AIR CRISP, set the temperature to 390°F, and set the time to 12 minutes. Select START/STOP to begin preheating.

9. When the unit beeps to signify it has preheated, coat the Crisper Basket with cooking spray and place the calzones in the basket. AIR CRISP for 10 to 12 minutes, until golden brown.

Grilled Vegetable Pizza

Servings: 2
Cooking Time: 10 Minutes

Ingredients:

- 2 tablespoons all-purpose flour, plus more as needed
- ½ store-bought pizza dough
- 1 tablespoon canola oil, divided
- ½ cup pizza sauce
- 1 cup shredded Mozzarella cheese
- ½ zucchini, thinly sliced
- ½ red onion, sliced
- ½ red bell pepper, seeded and thinly sliced

Directions:

1. Insert the Grill Grate and close the hood. Select GRILL, set the temperature to MAX, and set the time to 7 minutes. Select START/STOP to begin preheating.

2. While the unit is preheating, dust a clean work surface with the flour.

3. Place the dough on the floured surface and roll it into a 9-inch round of even thickness. Dust your rolling pin and work surface with additional flour, as needed, to ensure the dough does not stick.

4. Evenly brush the surface of the rolled-out dough with ½ tablespoon of oil. Flip the dough over and brush the other side with the remaining ½ tablespoon of oil. Poke the dough with a fork 5 or 6 times across its surface to prevent air pockets from forming while it cooks.

5. When the unit beeps to signify it has preheated, place the dough on the Grill Grate. Close the hood and GRILL for 4 minutes.

6. After 4 minutes, flip the dough, then spread the pizza sauce evenly over it. Sprinkle with the cheese, and top with the zucchini, onion, and pepper.

7. Close the hood and continue cooking for the remaining 2 to 3 minutes until the cheese is melted and the veggie slices begin to crisp.

8. When cooking is complete, let cool slightly before slicing.

Kidney Beans Oatmeal In Peppers

Servings: 2 To 4

Cooking Time: 6 Minutes

Ingredients:

- 2 large bell peppers, halved lengthwise, deseeded
- 2 tablespoons cooked kidney beans
- 2 tablespoons cooked chick peas
- 2 cups cooked oatmeal
- 1 teaspoon ground cumin
- ½ teaspoon paprika
- ½ teaspoon salt or to taste
- ¼ teaspoon black pepper powder
- ¼ cup yogurt

Directions:

1. Insert the Crisper Basket and close the hood. Select AIR CRISP, set the temperature to 355°F, and set the time to 6 minutes. Select START/STOP to begin preheating.
2. Put the bell peppers, cut-side down, in the Crisper Basket. Close the hood and AIR CRISP for 2 minutes.
3. Take the peppers out of the grill and let cool.
4. In a bowl, combine the rest of the ingredients.
5. Divide the mixture evenly and use each portion to stuff a pepper.
6. Return the stuffed peppers to the basket. Close the hood and AIR CRISP for 4 minutes.
7. Serve hot.

Poultry Recipes

Blackened Chicken Breasts

Servings: 4

Cooking Time: 20 Minutes

Ingredients:

- 1 large egg, beaten
- ¾ cup Blackened seasoning
- 2 whole boneless, skinless chicken breasts, halved
- Cooking spray

Directions:

1. Line the Crisper Basket with parchment paper.
2. Insert the Crisper Basket and close the hood. Select AIR CRISP, set the temperature to 360°F, and set the time to 20 minutes. Select START/STOP to begin preheating.
3. Place the beaten egg in one shallow bowl and the Blackened seasoning in another shallow bowl.
4. One at a time, dip the chicken pieces in the beaten egg and the Blackened seasoning, coating thoroughly.
5. Place the chicken pieces on the parchment and spritz with cooking spray.
6. Close the hood and AIR CRISP for 10 minutes. Flip the chicken, spritz it with cooking spray, and AIR CRISP for 10 minutes more until the internal temperature reaches 165°F and the chicken is no longer pink inside.
7. Let sit for 5 minutes before serving.

Crispy Chicken Strips

Servings: 4
Cooking Time: 20 Minutes

Ingredients:

- 1 tablespoon olive oil
- 1 pound boneless, skinless chicken tenderloins
- 1 teaspoon salt
- ½ teaspoon freshly ground black pepper
- ½ teaspoon paprika
- ½ teaspoon garlic powder
- ½ cup whole-wheat seasoned bread crumbs
- 1 teaspoon dried parsley
- Cooking spray

Directions:

1. Spray the Crisper Basket lightly with cooking spray.
2. Insert the Crisper Basket and close the hood. Select AIR CRISP, set the temperature to 370°F, and set the time to 20 minutes. Select START/STOP to begin preheating.
3. In a medium bowl, toss the chicken with the salt, pepper, paprika, and garlic powder until evenly coated.
4. Add the olive oil and toss to coat the chicken evenly.
5. In a separate, shallow bowl, mix together the bread crumbs and parsley.
6. Coat each piece of chicken evenly in the bread crumb mixture.
7. Place the chicken in the Crisper Basket in a single layer and spray it lightly with cooking spray. You may need to cook them in batches.
8. Close the hood and AIR CRISP for 10 minutes. Flip the chicken over, lightly spray it with cooking spray, and AIR CRISP for an additional 8 to 10 minutes, until golden brown. Serve.

Lemon And Rosemary Chicken

Servings: 4
Cooking Time: 15 Minutes

Ingredients:

- 3 pounds bone-in, skin-on chicken thighs
- 4 tablespoons avocado oil
- 2 tablespoons lemon-pepper seasoning
- 1 tablespoon chopped fresh rosemary
- 1 lemon, thinly sliced

Directions:

1. Insert the Grill Grate and close the hood. Select GRILL, set the temperature to LO, and set the time to 15 minutes. Select START/STOP to begin preheating.
2. Coat the chicken thighs with the avocado oil and rub the lemon-pepper seasoning and rosemary evenly over the chicken.
3. When the unit beeps to signify it has preheated, place the chicken thighs on the Grill Grate, skin-side up. Place the lemon slices on top of the chicken. Close the hood and grill for 8 minutes.
4. After 8 minutes, open the hood and remove the lemon slices. Flip the chicken and place the lemon slices back on top. Close the hood and cook for 7 minutes more.
5. When cooking is complete, remove the chicken from the grill and serve.

Honey Rosemary Chicken

Servings: 4

Cooking Time: 20 Minutes

Ingredients:

- ¼ cup balsamic vinegar
- ¼ cup honey
- 2 tablespoons olive oil
- 1 tablespoon dried rosemary leaves
- 1 teaspoon salt
- ½ teaspoon freshly ground black pepper
- 2 whole boneless, skinless chicken breasts, halved
- Cooking spray

Directions:

1. In a large resealable bag, combine the vinegar, honey, olive oil, rosemary, salt, and pepper. Add the chicken pieces, seal the bag, and refrigerate to marinate for at least 2 hours.
2. Insert the Crisper Basket and close the hood. Select BAKE, set the temperature to 325°F, and set the time to 20 minutes. Select START/STOP to begin preheating.
3. Line the Crisper Basket with parchment paper.
4. Remove the chicken from the marinade and place it on the parchment. Spritz with cooking spray.
5. Close the hood and BAKE for 10 minutes. Flip the chicken, spritz it with cooking spray, and bake for 10 minutes more until the internal temperature reaches 165°F and the chicken is no longer pink inside. Let sit for 5 minutes before serving.

Lime Chicken With Cilantro

Servings: 4

Cooking Time: 20 Minutes

Ingredients:

- 4 boneless, skinless chicken breasts
- ½ cup chopped fresh cilantro
- Juice of 1 lime
- Chicken seasoning or rub, to taste
- Salt and ground black pepper, to taste
- Cooking spray

Directions:

1. Put the chicken breasts in the large bowl, then add the cilantro, lime juice, chicken seasoning, salt, and black pepper. Toss to coat well.
2. Wrap the bowl in plastic and refrigerate to marinate for at least 30 minutes.
3. Spritz the Crisper Basket with cooking spray.
4. Insert the Crisper Basket and close the hood. Select AIR CRISP, set the temperature to 400°F, and set the time to 10 minutes. Select START/STOP to begin preheating.
5. Remove the marinated chicken breasts from the bowl and place in the preheated grill. Spritz with cooking spray. You may need to work in batches to avoid overcrowding.
6. Close the hood and AIR CRISP for 10 minutes or until the internal temperature of the chicken reaches at least 165°F. Flip the breasts halfway through.
7. Serve immediately.

Garlic Brown-butter Chicken With Tomatoes

Servings: 4
Cooking Time: 15 Minutes
Ingredients:
- 4 boneless, skinless chicken breasts
- Extra-virgin olive oil
- ½ teaspoon paprika
- ½ teaspoon sea salt
- 12 tablespoons (1½ sticks) unsalted butter
- 4 garlic cloves, minced
- 2 tablespoons light brown sugar, packed
- ½ teaspoon garlic powder
- 6 ounces cherry tomatoes

Directions:
1. Insert the Cooking Pot and close the hood. Select GRILL, set the temperature to MED, and set the time to 15 minutes. Select START/STOP to begin preheating.
2. While the unit is preheating, drizzle the chicken breasts with olive oil, then lightly sprinkle both sides with the paprika and salt.
3. When the unit beeps to signify it has preheated, place the butter and garlic in the Cooking Pot. Insert the Grill Grate on top and place the chicken breasts on the Grill Grate. Close the hood and grill for 8 minutes.
4. After 8 minutes, open the hood and use grill mitts to remove the Grill Grate and chicken. Add the brown sugar, garlic powder, and tomatoes to the butter and garlic and stir.
5. Transfer the chicken to the Cooking Pot, making sure you flip the breasts. Coat the chicken with the brown butter sauce. Close the hood and cook for 7 minutes more.
6. When cooking is complete, remove the chicken and place on a plate. Spoon the sauce over and serve.

Nutty Chicken Tenders

Servings: 4
Cooking Time: 12 Minutes
Ingredients:
- 1 pound chicken tenders
- 1 teaspoon kosher salt
- 1 teaspoon black pepper
- ½ teaspoon smoked paprika
- ¼ cup coarse mustard
- 2 tablespoons honey
- 1 cup finely crushed pecans

Directions:
1. Insert the Crisper Basket and close the hood. Select BAKE, set the temperature to 350°F, and set the time to 12 minutes. Select START/STOP to begin preheating.
2. Place the chicken in a large bowl. Sprinkle with the salt, pepper, and paprika. Toss until the chicken is coated with the spices. Add the mustard and honey and toss until the chicken is coated.
3. Place the pecans on a plate. Working with one piece of chicken at a time, roll the chicken in the pecans until both sides are coated. Lightly brush off any loose pecans. Place the chicken in the Crisper Basket.
4. Close the hood and BAKE for 12 minutes, or until the chicken is cooked through and the pecans are golden brown.
5. Serve warm.

Blackened Chicken

Servings: 4
Cooking Time: 10 Minutes
Ingredients:

- 1 tablespoon paprika
- 1 tablespoon garlic powder
- 1 tablespoon onion powder
- 1 tablespoon freshly ground black pepper
- 1 teaspoon Italian seasoning
- 1 teaspoon salt
- ½ teaspoon ground cumin
- ½ teaspoon cayenne pepper
- 4 tablespoons (½ stick) unsalted butter, melted
- ¼ cup avocado oil
- 4 boneless, skinless chicken breasts (about 2 pounds), halved crosswise

Directions:

1. Insert the Grill Grate and close the hood. Select GRILL, set the temperature to HI, and set the time to 10 minutes. Select START/STOP to begin preheating.
2. In a small bowl, combine the paprika, garlic powder, onion powder, black pepper, Italian seasoning, salt, cumin, and cayenne pepper.
3. In a separate small bowl, whisk together the butter and avocado oil. Lightly coat the chicken breasts on both sides with the butter-and-oil mixture, and then season both sides with the spice mix to get a nice coating.
4. When the unit beeps to signify it has preheated, open the hood and place the seasoned chicken on the Grill Grate. Close the hood and grill for 5 minutes.
5. After 5 minutes, open the hood and flip the chicken. Close the hood and cook for 5 minutes more.
6. When cooking is complete, remove the chicken from the grill and serve.

Roasted Cajun Turkey

Servings: 4
Cooking Time: 30 Minutes
Ingredients:

- 2 pounds turkey thighs, skinless and boneless
- 1 red onion, sliced
- 2 bell peppers, sliced
- 1 habanero pepper, minced
- 1 carrot, sliced
- 1 tablespoon Cajun seasoning mix
- 1 tablespoon fish sauce
- 2 cups chicken broth
- Nonstick cooking spray

Directions:

1. Select ROAST, set the temperature to 360°F, and set the time to 30 minutes. Select START/STOP to begin preheating.
2. Spritz the bottom and sides of the pot with nonstick cooking spray.
3. Arrange the turkey thighs in the pot. Add the onion, peppers, and carrot. Sprinkle with Cajun seasoning. Add the fish sauce and chicken broth.
4. Close the hood and ROAST for 30 minutes until cooked through. Serve warm.

Turkey Stuffed Bell Peppers

Servings: 4
Cooking Time: 15 Minutes
Ingredients:

- ½ pound lean ground turkey
- 4 medium bell peppers
- 1 can black beans, drained and rinsed
- 1 cup shredded reduced-fat Cheddar cheese
- 1 cup cooked long-grain brown rice
- 1 cup mild salsa
- 1¼ teaspoons chili powder
- 1 teaspoon salt
- ½ teaspoon ground cumin
- ½ teaspoon freshly ground black pepper
- Olive oil spray
- Chopped fresh cilantro, for garnish

Directions:

1. Insert the Crisper Basket and close the hood. Select AIR CRISP, set the temperature to 360°F, and set the time to 15 minutes. Select START/STOP to begin preheating.
2. In a large skillet over medium-high heat, cook the turkey, breaking it up with a spoon, until browned, about 5 minutes. Drain off any excess fat.
3. Cut about ½ inch off the tops of the peppers and then cut in half lengthwise. Remove and discard the seeds and set the peppers aside.
4. In a large bowl, combine the browned turkey, black beans, Cheddar cheese, rice, salsa, chili powder, salt, cumin, and black pepper. Spoon the mixture into the bell peppers.
5. Lightly spray the Crisper Basket with olive oil spray.
6. Place the stuffed peppers in the Crisper Basket. Close the hood and AIR CRISP for 10 to 15 minutes until heated through.
7. Garnish with cilantro and serve.

Mayonnaise-mustard Chicken

Servings: 4
Cooking Time: 15 Minutes
Ingredients:

- 6 tablespoons mayonnaise
- 2 tablespoons coarse-ground mustard
- 2 teaspoons honey (optional)
- 2 teaspoons curry powder
- 1 teaspoon kosher salt
- 1 teaspoon cayenne pepper
- 1 pound chicken tenders

Directions:

1. Insert the Crisper Basket and close the hood. Select BAKE, set the temperature to 350°F, and set the time to 15 minutes. Select START/STOP to begin preheating.
2. In a large bowl, whisk together the mayonnaise, mustard, honey (if using), curry powder, salt, and cayenne. Transfer half of the mixture to a serving bowl to serve as a dipping sauce. Add the chicken tenders to the large bowl and toss until well coated.
3. Place the tenders in the Crisper Basket. Close the hood and BAKE for 15 minutes. Use a meat thermometer to ensure the chicken has reached an internal temperature of 165°F.
4. Serve the chicken with the dipping sauce.

Spicy Chicken Kebabs

Servings: 4

Cooking Time: 14 Minutes

Ingredients:

- 1 tablespoon ground cumin
- 1 tablespoon garlic powder
- 1 tablespoon chili powder
- 2 teaspoons paprika
- ¼ teaspoon sea salt
- ¼ teaspoon freshly ground black pepper
- 1 pound boneless, skinless chicken breasts, cut in 2-inch cubes
- 2 tablespoons extra-virgin olive oil, divided
- 2 red bell peppers, seeded and cut into 1-inch cubes
- 1 red onion, quartered
- Juice of 1 lime

Directions:

1. In a small mixing bowl, combine the cumin, garlic powder, chili powder, paprika, salt, and pepper, and mix well.
2. Place the chicken, 1 tablespoon oil, and half of the spice mixture into a large resealable plastic bag or container. Toss to coat evenly.
3. Place the bell pepper, onion, remaining 1 tablespoon of oil, and remaining spice mixture into a large resealable plastic bag or container. Toss to coat evenly. Refrigerate the chicken and vegetables for at least 30 minutes.
4. Insert the Grill Grate and close the hood. Select GRILL, set the temperature to HIGH, and set the time to 14 minutes. Select START/STOP to begin preheating.
5. While the unit is preheating, assemble the kebabs by threading the chicken onto the wood skewers, alternating with the peppers and onion. Ensure the ingredients are pushed almost completely down to the end of the skewers.
6. When the unit beeps to signify it has preheated, place the skewers on the Grill Grate. Close the hood and GRILL for 10 to 14 minutes.
7. Cooking is complete when the internal temperature of the chicken reaches 165°F. When cooking is complete, remove from the heat, and drizzle with lime juice.

Strawberry-glazed Turkey

Servings: 2

Cooking Time: 37 Minutes

Ingredients:

- 2 pounds turkey breast
- 1 tablespoon olive oil
- Salt and ground black pepper, to taste
- 1 cup fresh strawberries

Directions:

1. Insert the Crisper Basket and close the hood. Select AIR CRISP, set the temperature to 375°F, and set the time to 37 minutes. Select START/STOP to begin preheating.
2. Rub the turkey bread with olive oil on a clean work surface, then sprinkle with salt and ground black pepper.
3. Transfer the turkey in the basket. Close the hood and AIR CRISP for 30 minutes or until the internal temperature of the turkey reaches at least 165°F. flip the turkey breast halfway through.
4. Meanwhile, put the strawberries in a food processor and pulse until smooth.
5. When the cooking of the turkey is complete, spread the puréed strawberries over the turkey. Close the hood and AIR CRISP for 7 more minutes.
6. Serve immediately.

Stuffed Spinach Chicken Breast

Servings: 6

Cooking Time: 12 Minutes

Ingredients:

- 6 ounces cream cheese, at room temperature
- 1 teaspoon salt
- ½ teaspoon freshly ground black pepper
- ¼ cup mayonnaise
- 2 teaspoons garlic powder
- ½ cup grated Parmesan cheese
- 3 cups loosely packed spinach
- 1 teaspoon red pepper flakes (optional)
- 6 (6- to 8-ounce) boneless, skinless chicken breasts, butterflied (see here)
- Avocado oil

Directions:

1. Insert the Grill Grate and close the hood. Select GRILL, set the temperature to HI, and set the time to 12 minutes. Select START/STOP to begin preheating.
2. While the unit is preheating, in a large bowl, combine the cream cheese, salt, pepper, mayonnaise, garlic powder, Parmesan cheese, spinach, and red pepper flakes (if using). Spread the mixture inside the chicken breasts evenly. Close the breasts (like a book), enclosing the stuffing. Drizzle both sides of the chicken breasts with avocado oil for a nice coating.
3. When the unit beeps to signify it has preheated, place the chicken breasts on the Grill Grate. Close the hood and grill for 6 minutes.
4. After 6 minutes, open the hood and flip the chicken. Close the hood and cook for 6 minutes more.
5. When cooking is complete, open the hood and remove the chicken breasts from the grill. Serve.

Spicy Bbq Chicken Drumsticks

Servings: 4

Cooking Time: 20 Minutes

Ingredients:

- 2 cups barbecue sauce
- Juice of 1 lime
- 2 tablespoons honey
- 1 tablespoon hot sauce
- Sea salt, to taste
- Freshly ground black pepper, to taste
- 1 pound chicken drumsticks

Directions:

1. In a large bowl, combine the barbecue sauce, lime juice, honey, and hot sauce. Season with salt and pepper. Set aside ½ cup of the sauce. Add the drumsticks to the bowl, and toss until evenly coated.
2. Insert the Grill Grate and close the hood. Select GRILL, set the temperature to MEDIUM, and set the time to 20 minutes. Select START/STOP to begin preheating.
3. When the unit beeps to signify it has preheated, place the drumsticks on the Grill Grate. Close the hood and GRILL for 18 minutes, basting often during cooking.
4. Cooking is complete when the internal temperature of the meat reaches at least 165°F on a food thermometer. If necessary, close the hood and continue grilling for 2 minutes more.

Adobo Chicken

Servings: 4
Cooking Time: 15 Minutes
Ingredients:

- 2 tablespoons soy sauce
- 2 tablespoons rice vinegar
- 1 tablespoon balsamic vinegar
- ¼ teaspoon freshly ground black pepper
- 4 garlic cloves, minced
- ½ teaspoon peeled minced fresh ginger
- Juice of ½ lemon
- ¼ teaspoon granulated sugar
- 3 bay leaves
- Pinch Italian seasoning (optional)
- Pinch ground cumin (optional)
- 3 pounds chicken drumsticks

Directions:

1. In a large bowl, whisk together the soy sauce, rice vinegar, balsamic vinegar, pepper, garlic, ginger, lemon juice, sugar, bay leaves, Italian seasoning (if using), and cumin (if using). Add the drumsticks to the marinade, making sure the meat is coated. Cover and refrigerate for at least 1 hour. If you have the time, marinate the chicken overnight to let all the flavors settle in.
2. Insert the Grill Grate and close the hood. Select GRILL, set the temperature to MED, and set the time to 15 minutes. Select START/STOP to begin preheating.
3. When the unit beeps to signify it has preheated, place the chicken drumsticks on the Grill Grate. Brush any leftover marinade onto the drumsticks. Close the hood and grill for 8 minutes.
4. After 8 minutes, open the hood and flip the drumsticks. Close the hood and continue cooking for 7 minutes more.
5. When cooking is complete, remove the drumsticks from the grill and serve.

Mini Turkey Meatloaves With Carrot

Servings: 4
Cooking Time: 20 To 24 Minutes
Ingredients:

- ⅓ cup minced onion
- ¼ cup grated carrot
- 2 garlic cloves, minced
- 2 tablespoons ground almonds
- 2 teaspoons olive oil
- 1 teaspoon dried marjoram
- 1 egg white
- ¾ pound ground turkey breast

Directions:

1. Select BAKE, set the temperature to 400°F, and set the time to 24 minutes. Select START/STOP to begin preheating.
2. In a medium bowl, stir together the onion, carrot, garlic, almonds, olive oil, marjoram, and egg white.
3. Add the ground turkey. With your hands, gently but thoroughly mix until combined.
4. Double 16 foil muffin cup liners to make 8 cups. Divide the turkey mixture evenly among the liners. Transfer to the pot.
5. Close the hood and BAKE for 20 to 24 minutes, or until the meatloaves reach an internal temperature of 165°F on a meat thermometer. Serve immediately.

Sweet Chili Turkey Kebabs

Servings: 4

Cooking Time: 12 Minutes

Ingredients:

- 2 pounds turkey breast, cut into 1-inch cubes
- ¼ cup honey
- 1 tablespoon extra-virgin olive oil
- 2 tablespoons apple cider vinegar
- 2 tablespoons soy sauce
- Juice of 1 lime
- 1 teaspoon red pepper flakes

Directions:

1. Place 5 or 6 turkey cubes on each of 8 to 10 skewers. In a zip-top bag, combine the honey, olive oil, vinegar, soy sauce, lime juice, and red pepper flakes. Shake to mix well. Place the turkey skewers in the marinade and massage to coat the meat. Seal the bag and let marinate at room temperature for 30 minutes or in the refrigerator overnight.

2. Insert the Grill Grate and close the hood. Select GRILL, set the temperature to MED, and set the time to 12 minutes. Select START/STOP to begin preheating.

3. When the unit beeps to signify it has preheated, place half of the skewers on the Grill Grate. Brush extra glaze on the skewers. Close the hood and grill for 3 minutes.

4. After 3 minutes, open the hood and flip the skewers. Close the hood and cook for 3 minutes more.

5. After 3 minutes, remove the skewers from the grill. Repeat steps 3 and 4 for the remaining skewers.

6. When cooking is complete, remove the kebabs from the grill and serve.

Grilled Cornish Hens

Servings: 4

Cooking Time: 20 Minutes

Ingredients:

- ½ cup avocado oil
- 1 teaspoon dried oregano
- ½ teaspoon freshly ground black pepper
- 1 teaspoon garlic salt
- 2 tablespoons minced garlic
- 1 teaspoon chopped fresh thyme
- 1 teaspoon chopped fresh parsley
- 1 teaspoon chopped fresh rosemary
- 2 (1-pound) Cornish hens
- 1 large yellow onion, halved
- 4 garlic cloves, peeled

Directions:

1. Plug the thermometer into the unit. Insert the Grill Grate and close the hood. Select GRILL, set the temperature to LO, then select PRESET. Use the arrows to the right to select CHICKEN. The unit will default to WELL to cook poultry to a safe temperature. Select START/STOP to begin preheating.

2. While the unit is preheating, place the Smart Thermometer into the thickest part of the breast of one of the hens. In a small bowl, whisk together the avocado oil, oregano, pepper, garlic salt, minced garlic, thyme, parsley, and rosemary. Cut a few small slits in the skin of each Cornish hen. Rub the seasoning oil all over the skin and between the skin and meat where you made the slits. Place an onion half and 2 garlic cloves inside the cavity of each hen.

3. When the unit beeps to signify it has preheated, place the hens on the Grill Grate. Close the hood and cook.

4. When the Foodi™ Grill tells you, open the hood and flip the hens. Close the hood and continue to cook.

5. When cooking is complete, remove the hens from the grill and let sit for 5 minutes. Serve.

Potato Cheese Crusted Chicken

Servings: 4
Cooking Time: 22 To 25 Minutes
Ingredients:

- ¼ cup buttermilk
- 1 large egg, beaten
- 1 cup instant potato flakes
- ¼ cup grated Parmesan cheese
- 1 teaspoon salt
- ½ teaspoon freshly ground black pepper
- 2 whole boneless, skinless chicken breasts, halved
- Cooking spray

Directions:

1. Insert the Crisper Basket and close the hood. Select BAKE, set the temperature to 325°F, and set the time to 25 minutes. Select START/STOP to begin preheating.
2. Line the Crisper Basket with parchment paper.
3. In a shallow bowl, whisk the buttermilk and egg until blended. In another shallow bowl, stir together the potato flakes, cheese, salt, and pepper.
4. One at a time, dip the chicken pieces in the buttermilk mixture and the potato flake mixture, coating thoroughly.
5. Place the coated chicken on the parchment and spritz with cooking spray.
6. Close the hood and BAKE for 15 minutes. Flip the chicken, spritz it with cooking spray, and bake for 7 to 10 minutes more until the outside is crispy and the inside is no longer pink. Serve immediately.

Roasted Chicken Tenders With Veggies

Servings: 4
Cooking Time: 18 To 20 Minutes
Ingredients:

- 1 pound chicken tenders
- 1 tablespoon honey
- Pinch salt
- Freshly ground black pepper, to taste
- ½ cup soft fresh bread crumbs
- ½ teaspoon dried thyme
- 1 tablespoon olive oil
- 2 carrots, sliced
- 12 small red potatoes

Directions:

1. Insert the Crisper Basket and close the hood. Select ROAST, set the temperature to 380°F, and set the time to 20 minutes. Select START/STOP to begin preheating.
2. In a medium bowl, toss the chicken tenders with the honey, salt, and pepper.
3. In a shallow bowl, combine the bread crumbs, thyme, and olive oil, and mix.
4. Coat the tenders in the bread crumbs, pressing firmly onto the meat.
5. Place the carrots and potatoes in the Crisper Basket and top with the chicken tenders.
6. Close the hood and ROAST for 18 to 20 minutes, or until the chicken is cooked to 165°F and the vegetables are tender, shaking the basket halfway during the cooking time.
7. Serve warm.

Crispy Dill Pickle Chicken Wings

Servings: 4
Cooking Time: 26 Minutes
Ingredients:

- 2 pounds bone-in chicken wings (drumettes and flats)
- 1½ cups dill pickle juice
- 1½ tablespoons vegetable oil
- ½ tablespoon dried dill
- ¾ teaspoon garlic powder
- Sea salt, to taste
- Freshly ground black pepper, to taste

Directions:

1. Place the chicken wings in a large shallow bowl. Pour the pickle juice over the top, ensuring all of the wings are coated and as submerged as possible. Cover and refrigerate for 2 hours.
2. Insert the Crisper Basket and close the hood. Select AIR CRISP, set the temperature to 390°F, and set the time to 26 minutes. Select START/STOP to begin preheating.
3. While the unit is preheating, rinse the brined chicken wings under cool water, then pat them dry with a paper towel. Place in a large bowl.
4. In a small bowl, whisk together the oil, dill, garlic powder, salt, and pepper. Drizzle over the wings and toss to fully coat them.
5. When the unit beeps to signify it has preheated, place the wings in the basket, spreading them out evenly. Close the hood and AIR CRISP for 11 minutes.
6. After 11 minutes, flip the wings with tongs. Close the hood and AIR CRISP for 11 minutes more.
7. Check the wings for doneness. Cooking is complete when the internal temperature of the chicken reaches at least 165°F on a food thermometer. If needed, AIR CRISP for up to 4 more minutes.
8. Remove the wings from the basket and serve immediately.

Rosemary Turkey Scotch Eggs

Servings: 4
Cooking Time: 12 Minutes
Ingredients:

- 1 egg
- 1 cup panko breadcrumbs
- ½ teaspoon rosemary
- 1 pound ground turkey
- 4 hard-boiled eggs, peeled
- Salt and ground black pepper, to taste
- Cooking spray

Directions:

1. Spritz the Crisper Basket with cooking spray.
2. Insert the Crisper Basket and close the hood. Select AIR CRISP, set the temperature to 400°F, and set the time to 12 minutes. Select START/STOP to begin preheating.
3. Whisk the egg with salt in a bowl. Combine the breadcrumbs with rosemary in a shallow dish.
4. Stir the ground turkey with salt and ground black pepper in a separate large bowl, then divide the ground turkey into four portions.
5. Wrap each hard-boiled egg with a portion of ground turkey. Dredge in the whisked egg, then roll over the breadcrumb mixture.
6. Place the wrapped eggs in the basket and spritz with cooking spray. Close the hood and AIR CRISP for 12 minutes or until golden brown and crunchy. Flip the eggs halfway through.
7. Serve immediately.

Herbed Grilled Chicken Thighs

Servings: 4
Cooking Time: 13 Minutes
Ingredients:

- Grated zest of 2 lemons
- Juice of 2 lemons
- 3 sprigs fresh rosemary, leaves finely chopped
- 3 sprigs fresh sage, leaves finely chopped
- 2 garlic cloves, minced
- ¼ teaspoon red pepper flakes
- ¼ cup canola oil
- Sea salt
- 4 boneless chicken thighs

Directions:

1. In a small bowl, whisk together the lemon zest and juice, rosemary, sage, garlic, red pepper flakes, and oil. Season with salt.
2. Place the chicken and lemon-herb mixture in a large resealable plastic bag or container. Toss to coat evenly. Refrigerate the chicken for at least 30 minutes.
3. Insert the Grill Grate and close the hood. Select GRILL, set the temperature to HIGH, and set the time to 13 minutes. Select START/STOP to begin preheating.
4. When the unit beeps to signify it has preheated, place the chicken on the Grill Grate. Close the hood and GRILL for 10 to 13 minutes.
5. Cooking is complete when the internal temperature of the chicken reaches at least 165°F on a food thermometer.

Fried Buffalo Chicken Taquitos

Servings: 6
Cooking Time: 5 To 10 Minutes
Ingredients:

- 8 ounces fat-free cream cheese, softened
- ⅛ cup Buffalo sauce
- 2 cups shredded cooked chicken
- 12 low-carb flour tortillas
- Olive oil spray

Directions:

1. Spray the Crisper Basket lightly with olive oil spray.
2. Insert the Crisper Basket and close the hood. Select AIR CRISP, set the temperature to 360°F, and set the time to 10 minutes. Select START/STOP to begin preheating.
3. In a large bowl, mix together the cream cheese and Buffalo sauce until well combined. Add the chicken and stir until combined.
4. Place the tortillas on a clean workspace. Spoon 2 to 3 tablespoons of the chicken mixture in a thin line down the center of each tortilla. Roll up the tortillas.
5. Place the tortillas in the Crisper Basket, seam-side down. Spray each tortilla lightly with olive oil spray. You may need to cook the taquitos in batches.
6. Close the hood and AIR CRISP for 5 to 10 minutes until golden brown.
7. Serve hot.

Buttermilk Ranch Chicken Tenders

Servings: 4
Cooking Time: 10 Minutes
Ingredients:

- 2 cups buttermilk
- 1 (0.4-ounce) packet ranch seasoning mix
- 1½ pounds boneless, skinless chicken breasts (about 3 breasts), cut into 1-inch strips
- 2 cups all-purpose flour
- ¼ teaspoon paprika
- ¼ teaspoon garlic powder
- ¼ teaspoon baking powder
- 2 teaspoons salt
- 2 large eggs
- ¼ cup avocado oil, divided

Directions:

1. In a large bowl, whisk together the buttermilk and ranch seasoning. Place the chicken strips in the bowl. Cover and let marinate in the refrigerator for 30 minutes.

2. Create an assembly line with 2 large bowls. Combine the flour, paprika, garlic powder, baking powder, and salt in one bowl. In the other bowl, whisk together the eggs. One at a time, remove the chicken strips from the marinade, shaking off any excess liquid. Dredge the chicken strip in the seasoned flour, coating both sides, then dip it in the beaten egg. Finally, dip it back into the seasoned flour bowl again. Shake any excess flour off. Repeat the process with all the chicken strips, setting them aside on a flat tray or plate once coated.

3. Insert the Grill Grate and close the hood. Select GRILL, set the temperature to MED, and set the time to 10 minutes. Select START/STOP to begin preheating.

4. While the unit is preheating, use a basting brush to generously coat one side of the chicken strips with half of the avocado oil.

5. When the unit beeps to signify it has preheated, place the chicken strips on the grill, oiled-side down. Brush the top of the chicken strips with the rest of the avocado oil. Close the hood and grill for 5 minutes.

6. After 5 minutes, open the hood and flip the chicken strips. Close the hood and continue cooking for 5 minutes more.

7. When cooking is complete, the chicken strips will be golden brown and crispy. Remove them from the grill and serve.

Simple Whole Chicken Bake

Servings: 2 To 4
Cooking Time: 1 Hour
Ingredients:

- ½ cup melted butter
- 3 tablespoons garlic, minced
- Salt, to taste
- 1 teaspoon ground black pepper
- 1 whole chicken

Directions:

1. Select BAKE, set the temperature to 350°F, and set the time to 1 hour. Select START/STOP to begin preheating.
2. Combine the butter with garlic, salt, and ground black pepper in a small bowl.
3. Brush the butter mixture over the whole chicken, then place the chicken in a baking pan, skin side down.
4. Place the pan directly in the pot. Close the hood and BAKE for 1 hour, or until an instant-read thermometer inserted in the thickest part of the chicken registers at least 165°F. Flip the chicken halfway through.
5. Remove the chicken from the grill and allow to cool for 15 minutes before serving.

Orange And Honey Glazed Duck With Apples

Servings: 2 To 3

Cooking Time: 15 Minutes

Ingredients:

- 1 pound duck breasts
- Kosher salt and pepper, to taste
- Juice and zest of 1 orange
- ¼ cup honey
- 2 sprigs thyme, plus more for garnish
- 2 firm tart apples, such as Fuji

Directions:

1. Insert the Crisper Basket and close the hood. Select ROAST, set the temperature to 400°F, and set the time to 13 minutes. Select START/STOP to begin preheating.

2. Pat the duck breasts dry and, using a sharp knife, make 3 to 4 shallow, diagonal slashes in the skin. Turn the breasts and score the skin on the diagonal in the opposite direction to create a cross-hatch pattern. Season well with salt and pepper.

3. Place the duck breasts skin-side up in the Crisper Basket. Close the hood and ROAST for 8 minutes. Flip and roast for 4 more minutes on the second side.

4. While the duck is roasting, prepare the sauce. Combine the orange juice and zest, honey, and thyme in a small saucepan. Bring to a boil, stirring to dissolve the honey, then reduce the heat and simmer until thickened. Core the apples and cut into quarters. Cut each quarter into 3 or 4 slices depending on the size.

5. After the duck has cooked on both sides, turn it and brush the skin with the orange-honey glaze. Roast for 1 more minute. Remove the duck breasts to a cutting board and allow to rest.

6. Toss the apple slices with the remaining orange-honey sauce in a medium bowl. Arrange the apples in a single layer in the Crisper Basket. AIR CRISP for 10 minutes while the duck breast rests. Slice the duck breasts on the bias and divide them and the apples among 2 or 3 plates.

7. Serve warm, garnished with additional thyme.

Spiced Turkey Tenderloin

Servings: 4

Cooking Time: 30 Minutes

Ingredients:

- ½ teaspoon paprika
- ½ teaspoon garlic powder
- ½ teaspoon salt
- ½ teaspoon freshly ground black pepper
- Pinch cayenne pepper
- 1½ pounds turkey breast tenderloin
- Olive oil spray

Directions:

1. Spray the Crisper Basket lightly with olive oil spray.

2. Insert the Crisper Basket and close the hood. Select AIR CRISP, set the temperature to 370°F, and set the time to 30 minutes. Select START/STOP to begin preheating.

3. In a small bowl, combine the paprika, garlic powder, salt, black pepper, and cayenne pepper. Rub the mixture all over the turkey.

4. Place the turkey in the Crisper Basket and lightly spray with olive oil spray.

5. Close the hood and AIR CRISP for 15 minutes. Flip the turkey over and lightly spray with olive oil spray. AIR CRISP until the internal temperature reaches at least 170°F for an additional 10 to 15 minutes.

6. Let the turkey rest for 10 minutes before slicing and serving.

Chicken Cordon Bleu Roll-ups

Servings: 4

Cooking Time: 15 Minutes

Ingredients:

- 1 tablespoon garlic powder
- 1 tablespoon onion powder
- 1½ pounds boneless, skinless chicken breasts (about 3 breasts)
- 6 ounces thin-sliced deli ham
- 6 ounces Swiss cheese, sliced
- 2 large eggs
- 1 cup plain bread crumbs
- ¼ cup sour cream
- 3 tablespoons Dijon mustard
- ¼ teaspoon granulated sugar or honey

Directions:

1. Insert the Grill Grate and close the hood. Select GRILL, set the temperature to MED, and set the time to 15 minutes. Select START/STOP to begin preheating.

2. In a small bowl, combine the garlic powder and onion powder.

3. Cut each chicken breast in half from the side (parallel to the cutting board) to create 6 thinner, flatter chicken breasts. Lightly coat the chicken all over with the garlic-and-onion mixture.

4. Layer 3 or 4 slices of ham on top of each piece of chicken, and top with about 1 ounce of cheese. Starting at the short end, roll the chicken breasts to wrap the ham and cheese inside. Secure the chicken roll-ups with toothpicks.

5. In a large bowl, whisk the eggs. Put the bread crumbs in a separate large bowl. Dip the chicken roll-ups in the egg and then into the bread crumbs until fully coated.

6. When the unit beeps to signify it has preheated, place the roll-ups on the Grill Grate. Close the hood and grill for 7 minutes, 30 seconds.

7. After 7 minutes, 30 seconds, open the hood and flip the roll-ups. Close the hood and continue cooking for 7 minutes, 30 seconds more.

8. While the roll-ups are cooking, in a small bowl, combine the sour cream, Dijon mustard, and sugar and stir until the sugar is dissolved.

9. When cooking is complete, remove the roll-ups from the grill and serve with the sauce, for dipping.

Sauces, Dips, And Dressings Recipes

Lemon Dijon Vinaigrette

Servings:6
Cooking Time: 0 Minutes
Ingredients:
- ¼ cup extra-virgin olive oil
- 1 garlic clove, minced
- 2 tablespoons freshly squeezed lemon juice
- 1 teaspoon Dijon mustard
- ½ teaspoon raw honey
- ¼ teaspoon salt
- ¼ teaspoon dried basil

Directions:
1. Place all the ingredients in a mason jar. Cover and shake vigorously until thoroughly mixed and well emulsified.
2. Serve chilled.

Cashew Pesto

Servings:1
Cooking Time: 0 Minutes
Ingredients:
- ¼ cup raw cashews
- Juice of 1 lemon
- 2 garlic cloves
- ⅓ red onion
- 1 tablespoon olive oil
- 4 cups basil leaves, packed
- 1 cup wheatgrass
- ¼ cup water
- ¼ teaspoon salt

Directions:
1. Put the cashews in a heatproof bowl and add boiling water to cover. Soak for 5 minutes and then drain.
2. Put all ingredients in a blender and blend for 2 to 3 minutes or until fully combined.

Sides, Snacks & Appetizers Recipes

Garlic Fries

Servings: 4
Cooking Time: 20 Minutes
Ingredients:
- 2 large Idaho or russet potatoes (1½ to 2 pounds)
- 1 head garlic (10 to 12 cloves)
- 4 tablespoons avocado oil, divided
- 1 teaspoon sea salt
- Chopped fresh parsley, for garnish

Directions:
1. Cut the potatoes into ¼-inch-thick slices. Place the slices in a large bowl and cover with cold water. Set aside for 30 minutes. This will ensure the potatoes cook well and crisp up perfectly. While the potatoes are soaking, mince the garlic cloves.
2. Drain the potatoes and pat dry using paper towels. In a large bowl, toss the potato slices with 2 tablespoons of avocado oil.
3. Insert the Cooking Pot and Crisper Basket and close the hood. Select AIR CRISP, set the temperature to 390°F, and set the time to 20 minutes. Select START/STOP to begin preheating.
4. While the unit is preheating, in a small bowl, combine the remaining 2 tablespoons of avocado oil with the minced garlic.
5. When the unit beeps to signify it has preheated, put the fries in the Crisper Basket. Close the hood and cook for 10 minutes.
6. After 10 minutes, open the hood and give the basket a shake to toss the fries. Close the hood and continue cooking for 5 minutes. Open the hood again and give the basket a shake. Close the hood and cook for 5 minutes more.
7. When cooking is complete, the fries will be crispy and golden brown. If you like them extra-crispy, continue cooking to your liking. Transfer the fries to a large bowl and drizzle with the garlic oil. Toss and season with the salt. Garnish with the parsley and serve.

Mozzarella Sticks

Servings: 4
Cooking Time: 8 Minutes
Ingredients:
- 2 large eggs
- 2 cups plain bread crumbs
- 2 tablespoons Italian seasoning
- 10 to 12 mozzarella cheese sticks
- Marinara sauce, for dipping

Directions:
1. In a large bowl, whisk the eggs. In a separate large bowl, combine the bread crumbs and Italian seasoning.
2. Dip each cheese stick in the egg and then dip it in the bread crumbs to evenly coat. Place the breaded mozzarella sticks on a baking sheet or flat tray, then freeze for 30 minutes.
3. Insert the Grill Grate and close the hood. Select GRILL, set the temperature to MED, and set the time to 8 minutes. Select START/STOP to begin preheating.
4. When the unit beeps to signify it has preheated, open the hood and place the mozzarella sticks on the Grill Grate. Close the hood and grill for 8 minutes.
5. When cooking is complete, the mozzarella sticks will be golden brown and crispy. If you prefer browner mozzarella sticks, continue cooking to your liking. Serve with the marinara sauce on the side.

Blt With Grilled Heirloom Tomato

Servings: 4

Cooking Time: 10 Minutes

Ingredients:

- 8 slices white bread
- 8 tablespoons mayonnaise
- 2 heirloom tomatoes, sliced ¼-inch thick
- 2 tablespoons canola oil
- Sea salt, to taste
- Freshly ground black pepper, to taste
- 8 slices bacon, cooked
- 8 leaves iceberg lettuce

Directions:

1. Insert the Grill Grate, and close the hood. Select GRILL, set the temperature to MAX, and set the time to 10 minutes. Select START/STOP to begin preheating.

2. While the unit is preheating, spread a thin layer of mayonnaise on one side of each piece of bread.

3. When the unit beeps to signify it has preheated, place the bread, mayonnaise-side down, on the Grill Grate. Close the hood and GRILL for 2 to 3 minutes, until crisp.

4. Meanwhile, remove the watery pulp and seeds from the tomato slices. Brush both sides of the tomatoes with the oil and season with salt and pepper.

5. After 2 to 3 minutes, remove the bread and place the tomatoes on the grill. Close the hood and continue grilling for the remaining 6 to 8 minutes.

6. To assemble, spread a thin layer of mayonnaise on the non-grilled sides of the bread. Layer the tomatoes, bacon, and lettuce on the bread, and top with the remaining slices of bread. Slice each sandwich in half and serve.

Cayenne Sesame Nut Mix

Servings:4

Cooking Time: 2 Minutes

Ingredients:

- 1 tablespoon buttery spread, melted
- 2 teaspoons honey
- ¼ teaspoon cayenne pepper
- 2 teaspoons sesame seeds
- ¼ teaspoon kosher salt
- ¼ teaspoon freshly ground black pepper
- 1 cup cashews
- 1 cup almonds
- 1 cup mini pretzels
- 1 cup rice squares cereal
- Cooking spray

Directions:

1. Select BAKE, set the temperature to 360°F, and set the time to 2 minutes. Select START/STOP to begin preheating.

2. In a large bowl, combine the buttery spread, honey, cayenne pepper, sesame seeds, kosher salt, and black pepper, then add the cashews, almonds, pretzels, and rice squares, tossing to coat.

3. Spray a baking pan with cooking spray, then pour the mixture into the pan. Place the pan directly in the pot. Close the hood and BAKE for 2 minutes.

4. Remove the sesame mix from the grill and allow to cool in the pan on a wire rack for 5 minutes before serving.

Dill Pickles

Servings: 4
Cooking Time: 10 Minutes
Ingredients:
- 20 dill pickle slices
- ¼ cup all-purpose flour
- ⅛ teaspoon baking powder
- 3 tablespoons beer or seltzer water
- ⅛ teaspoon sea salt
- 2 tablespoons water, plus more if needed
- 2 tablespoons cornstarch
- 1½ cups panko bread crumbs
- 1 teaspoon paprika
- 1 teaspoon garlic powder
- ¼ teaspoon cayenne pepper
- 2 tablespoons canola oil, divided

Directions:
1. Pat the pickle slices dry, and place them on a dry plate in the freezer.
2. In a medium bowl, stir together the flour, baking powder, beer, salt, and water. The batter should be the consistency of cake batter. If it is too thick, add more water, 1 teaspoon at a time.
3. Place the cornstarch in a small shallow bowl.
4. In a separate large shallow bowl, combine the bread crumbs, paprika, garlic powder, and cayenne pepper.
5. Remove the pickles from the freezer. Dredge each one in cornstarch. Tap off any excess, then coat in the batter. Lastly, coat evenly with the bread crumb mixture.
6. Insert the Crisper Basket and close the hood. Select AIR CRISP, set the temperature to 360°F, and set the time to 10 minutes. Select START/STOP to begin preheating.
7. When the unit beeps to signify it has preheated, place the breaded pickles in the basket, stacking them if necessary, and gently brush them with 1 tablespoon of oil. Close the hood and AIR CRISP for 5 minutes.
8. After 5 minutes, shake the basket and gently brush the pickles with the remaining 1 tablespoon of oil. Place the basket back in the unit and close the hood to resume cooking.
9. When cooking is complete, serve immediately.

Roasted Mixed Nuts

Servings: 6
Cooking Time: 20 Minutes
Ingredients:
- 2 cups mixed nuts (walnuts, pecans, and almonds)
- 2 tablespoons egg white
- 2 tablespoons sugar
- 1 teaspoon paprika
- 1 teaspoon ground cinnamon
- Cooking spray

Directions:
1. Spray the Crisper Basket with cooking spray.
2. Insert the Crisper Basket and close the hood. Select ROAST, set the temperature to 300°F, and set the time to 20 minutes. Select START/STOP to begin preheating.
3. Stir together the mixed nuts, egg white, sugar, paprika, and cinnamon in a small bowl until the nuts are fully coated.
4. Put the nuts in the Crisper Basket. Close the hood and ROAST for 20 minutes. Shake the basket halfway through the cooking time for even cooking.
5. Transfer the nuts to a bowl and serve warm.

Homemade Bbq Chicken Pizza

Servings: 1
Cooking Time: 8 Minutes
Ingredients:

- 1 piece naan bread
- ¼ cup Barbecue sauce
- ¼ cup shredded Monterrey Jack cheese
- ¼ cup shredded Mozzarella cheese
- ½ chicken herby sausage, sliced
- 2 tablespoons red onion, thinly sliced
- Chopped cilantro or parsley, for garnish
- Cooking spray

Directions:

1. Insert the Crisper Basket and close the hood. Select AIR CRISP, set the temperature to 400°F, and set the time to 8 minutes. Select START/STOP to begin preheating.
2. Spritz the bottom of naan bread with cooking spray, then transfer to the Crisper Basket.
3. Brush with the Barbecue sauce. Top with the cheeses, sausage, and finish with the red onion.
4. Close the hood and AIR CRISP for 8 minutes until the cheese is melted.
5. Garnish with the chopped cilantro or parsley before slicing to serve.

Cheesy Apple Roll-ups

Servings:8
Cooking Time: 4 To 5 Minutes
Ingredients:

- 8 slices whole wheat sandwich bread
- 4 ounces Colby Jack cheese, grated
- ½ small apple, chopped
- 2 tablespoons butter, melted

Directions:

1. Insert the Crisper Basket and close the hood. Select AIR CRISP, set the temperature to 390°F, and set the time to 5 minutes. Select START/STOP to begin preheating.
2. Remove the crusts from the bread and flatten the slices with a rolling pin. Don't be gentle. Press hard so that bread will be very thin.
3. Top bread slices with cheese and chopped apple, dividing the ingredients evenly.
4. Roll up each slice tightly and secure each with one or two toothpicks.
5. Brush outside of rolls with melted butter.
6. Place in the Crisper Basket. Close the hood and AIR CRISP for 4 to 5 minutes, or until outside is crisp and nicely browned.
7. Serve hot.

Bacon-wrapped Onion Rings And Spicy Aioli

Servings: 4

Cooking Time: 10 Minutes

Ingredients:

- For the onion rings
- 3 large white onions
- 2 (1-pound) packages thin-sliced bacon
- For the spicy garlic aioli sauce
- 1 cup mayonnaise
- ¼ teaspoon garlic powder
- 1 tablespoon sriracha
- 1 teaspoon freshly squeezed lemon juice

Directions:

1. Insert the Grill Grate and close the hood. Select GRILL, set the temperature to MED, and set the time to 10 minutes. Select START/STOP to begin preheating.

2. While the unit is preheating, cut both ends off the onions. Slice each onion crosswise into thirds and peel off the outer layer of onion skin. Separate the onion rings, keeping two onion layers together to have a stable and firm ring. Wrap each onion ring pair with a slice of bacon. The bacon should slightly overlap itself as you wrap it all the way around the onion ring. Larger rings may need 2 slices of bacon.

3. When the unit beeps to signify it has preheated, place the onion rings on the Grill Grate. Close the hood and grill for 10 minutes. Flipping is not necessary.

4. When cooking is complete, the bacon will be cooked through and starting to crisp. If you prefer the bacon crispier or even close to charred, continue cooking to your liking.

5. While the onion rings are cooking, in a small bowl, whisk together the mayonnaise, garlic powder, sriracha, and lemon juice. Use more or less sriracha depending on your preferred spice level. Serve with the bacon onion rings.

Cheesy Crab Toasts

Servings:15

Cooking Time: 5 Minutes

Ingredients:

- 1 can flaked crab meat, well drained
- 3 tablespoons light mayonnaise
- ¼ cup shredded Parmesan cheese
- ¼ cup shredded Cheddar cheese
- 1 teaspoon Worcestershire sauce
- ½ teaspoon lemon juice
- 1 loaf artisan bread, French bread, or baguette, cut into ⅜-inch-thick slices

Directions:

1. Insert the Crisper Basket and close the hood. Select BAKE, set the temperature to 360°F, and set the time to 5 minutes. Select START/STOP to begin preheating.

2. In a large bowl, stir together all the ingredients except the bread slices.

3. On a clean work surface, lay the bread slices. Spread ½ tablespoon of crab mixture onto each slice of bread.

4. Arrange the bread slices in the Crisper Basket in a single layer. You'll need to work in batches to avoid overcrowding.

5. Close the hood and BAKE for 5 minutes until the tops are lightly browned.

6. Transfer to a plate and repeat with the remaining bread slices.

7. Serve warm.

Easy Muffuletta Sliders With Olives

Servings:8
Cooking Time: 5 To 7 Minutes
Ingredients:

- ¼ pound thinly sliced deli ham
- ¼ pound thinly sliced pastrami
- 4 ounces low-fat Mozzarella cheese, grated
- 8 slider buns, split in half
- Cooking spray
- 1 tablespoon sesame seeds
- Olive Mix:
- ½ cup sliced green olives with pimentos
- ¼ cup sliced black olives
- ¼ cup chopped kalamata olives
- 1 teaspoon red wine vinegar
- ¼ teaspoon basil
- ⅛ teaspoon garlic powder

Directions:

1. Insert the Crisper Basket and close the hood. Select BAKE, set the temperature to 360°F, and set the time to 7 minutes. Select START/STOP to begin preheating.
2. Combine all the ingredients for the olive mix in a small bowl and stir well.
3. Stir together the ham, pastrami, and cheese in a medium bowl and divide the mixture into 8 equal portions.
4. Assemble the sliders: Top each bottom bun with 1 portion of meat and cheese, 2 tablespoons of olive mix, finished by the remaining buns. Lightly spritz the tops with cooking spray. Scatter the sesame seeds on top.
5. Working in batches, arrange the sliders in the Crisper Basket. Close the hood and BAKE for 5 to 7 minutes until the cheese melts.
6. Transfer to a large plate and repeat with the remaining sliders.
7. Serve immediately.

Rosemary Baked Cashews

Servings:2
Cooking Time: 3 Minutes
Ingredients:

- 2 sprigs of fresh rosemary
- 1 teaspoon olive oil
- 1 teaspoon kosher salt
- ½ teaspoon honey
- 2 cups roasted and unsalted whole cashews
- Cooking spray

Directions:

1. Insert the Crisper Basket and close the hood. Select BAKE, set the temperature to 300°F, and set the time to 3 minutes. Select START/STOP to begin preheating.
2. In a medium bowl, whisk together the chopped rosemary, olive oil, kosher salt, and honey. Set aside.
3. Spray the Crisper Basket with cooking spray, then place the cashews and the whole rosemary sprig in the basket. Close the hood and BAKE for 3 minutes.
4. Remove the cashews and rosemary from the grill, then discard the rosemary and add the cashews to the olive oil mixture, tossing to coat.
5. Allow to cool for 15 minutes before serving.

One-pot Nachos

Servings: 4
Cooking Time: 10 Minutes
Ingredients:
- 1 pound ground beef
- 1 (1-ounce) packet taco seasoning mix
- 1 (16-ounce) can refried beans
- 1 (14.5-ounce) can diced tomatoes, drained
- 2 cups sour cream
- 3 cups shredded Mexican cheese blend
- 2 cups shredded iceberg lettuce
- 1 cup sliced black olives
- Sliced scallions, both white and green parts, for garnish
- 1 (10- to 13-ounce) bag tortilla chips

Directions:
1. Insert the Cooking Pot and close the hood. Select GRILL, set the temperature to MED, and set the time to 10 minutes. Select START/STOP to begin preheating.
2. When the unit beeps to signify it has preheated, place the ground beef in the Cooking Pot and sprinkle it with the taco seasoning. Using a wooden spoon or spatula, break apart the ground beef. Close the hood and cook for 5 minutes.
3. After 5 minutes, open the hood and stir the ground beef to mix a little more with the taco seasoning. Evenly spread the ground beef across the bottom of the pot. Add the refried beans in an even layer over the meat, then an even layer of the diced tomatoes. Close the hood and cook for 5 minutes more.
4. When cooking is complete, remove the Cooking Pot from the unit and place it on a heatproof surface. Add an even layer each of sour cream, shredded cheese, shredded lettuce, and olives on top. Garnish with scallions and serve with the tortilla chips.

Candied Brussels Sprouts With Bacon

Servings: 4
Cooking Time: 20 Minutes
Ingredients:
- 2 pounds Brussels sprouts, ends trimmed
- 2 tablespoons avocado oil
- ¼ cup light brown sugar, packed
- 8 ounces thick-cut bacon, cut into bite-size pieces
- 3 tablespoons maple syrup

Directions:
1. Insert the Crisper Basket and close the hood. Select AIR CRISP, set the temperature to 390°F, and set the time to 20 minutes. Select START/STOP to begin preheating.
2. While the unit is preheating, put the Brussels sprouts in a large bowl, drizzle with the avocado oil, and toss to coat.
3. In a medium bowl, rub the brown sugar into the bacon pieces.
4. When the unit beeps to signify it has preheated, place the Brussels sprouts in the Crisper Basket and sprinkle the bacon bits on top. Close the hood and cook for 10 minutes.
5. After 10 minutes, open the hood and flip the Brussels sprouts. Drizzle the maple syrup over the sprouts. Close the hood and cook for 10 minutes more. If you like, you can turn the Brussels sprouts a second time when there are 5 minutes of cooking time remaining.
6. When cooking is complete, remove the Brussels sprouts from the grill and serve. If you want your Brussels sprouts crispier and more browned, continue cooking to your liking.

Breaded Green Olives

Servings: 4
Cooking Time: 8 Minutes
Ingredients:

- 1 jar pitted green olives
- ½ cup all-purpose flour
- Salt and pepper, to taste
- ½ cup bread crumbs
- 1 egg
- Cooking spray

Directions:

1. Insert the Crisper Basket and close the hood. Select AIR CRISP, set the temperature to 400°F, and set the time to 8 minutes. Select START/STOP to begin preheating.
2. Remove the olives from the jar and dry thoroughly with paper towels.
3. In a small bowl, combine the flour with salt and pepper to taste. Place the bread crumbs in another small bowl. In a third small bowl, beat the egg.
4. Spritz the Crisper Basket with cooking spray.
5. Dip the olives in the flour, then the egg, and then the bread crumbs.
6. Place the breaded olives in the basket. It is okay to stack them. Spray the olives with cooking spray. Close the hood and AIR CRISP for 6 minutes. Flip the olives and AIR CRISP for an additional 2 minutes, or until brown and crisp.
7. Cool before serving.

Cuban Sandwiches

Servings:4
Cooking Time: 8 Minutes
Ingredients:

- 8 slices ciabatta bread, about ¼-inch thick
- Cooking spray
- 1 tablespoon brown mustard
- Toppings:
- 6 to 8 ounces thinly sliced leftover roast pork
- 4 ounces thinly sliced deli turkey
- ⅓ cup bread and butter pickle slices
- 2 to 3 ounces Pepper Jack cheese slices

Directions:

1. Insert the Crisper Basket and close the hood. Select AIR CRISP, set the temperature to 390°F, and set the time to 8 minutes. Select START/STOP to begin preheating.
2. On a clean work surface, spray one side of each slice of bread with cooking spray. Spread the other side of each slice of bread evenly with brown mustard.
3. Top 4 of the bread slices with the roast pork, turkey, pickle slices, cheese, and finish with remaining bread slices. Transfer to the Crisper Basket.
4. Close the hood and AIR CRISP for 8 minutes until golden brown.
5. Cool for 5 minutes and serve warm.

Caramelized Peaches

Servings: 4
Cooking Time: 10 To 13 Minutes
Ingredients:
- 2 tablespoons sugar
- ¼ teaspoon ground cinnamon
- 4 peaches, cut into wedges
- Cooking spray

Directions:
1. Lightly spray the Crisper Basket with cooking spray.
2. Insert the Crisper Basket and close the hood. Select AIR CRISP, set the temperature to 350°F, and set the time to 13 minutes. Select START/STOP to begin preheating.
3. Toss the peaches with the sugar and cinnamon in a medium bowl until evenly coated.
4. Arrange the peaches in the Crisper Basket in a single layer. Lightly mist the peaches with cooking spray. You may need to work in batches to avoid overcrowding.
5. Close the hood and AIR CRISP for 5 minutes. Flip the peaches and AIR CRISP for another 5 to 8 minutes, or until the peaches are caramelized.
6. Repeat with the remaining peaches.
7. Let the peaches cool for 5 minutes and serve warm.

Bruschetta With Tomato And Basil

Servings: 6
Cooking Time: 6 Minutes
Ingredients:
- 4 tomatoes, diced
- ⅓ cup shredded fresh basil
- ¼ cup shredded Parmesan cheese
- 1 tablespoon balsamic vinegar
- 1 tablespoon minced garlic
- 1 teaspoon olive oil
- 1 teaspoon salt
- 1 teaspoon freshly ground black pepper
- 1 loaf French bread, cut into 1-inch-thick slices
- Cooking spray

Directions:
1. Insert the Crisper Basket and close the hood. Select BAKE, set the temperature to 250°F, and set the time to 3 minutes. Select START/STOP to begin preheating.
2. Mix together the tomatoes and basil in a medium bowl. Add the cheese, vinegar, garlic, olive oil, salt, and pepper and stir until well incorporated. Set aside.
3. Spritz the Crisper Basket with cooking spray. Working in batches, lay the bread slices in the basket in a single layer. Spray the slices with cooking spray.
4. Close the hood and BAKE for 3 minutes until golden brown.
5. Remove from the basket to a plate. Repeat with the remaining bread slices.
6. Top each slice with a generous spoonful of the tomato mixture and serve.

Grilled Carrots With Honey Glazed

Servings: 4
Cooking Time: 10 Minutes

Ingredients:

- 6 medium carrots, peeled and cut lengthwise
- 1 tablespoon canola oil
- 2 tablespoons unsalted butter, melted
- ¼ cup brown sugar, melted
- ¼ cup honey
- ⅛ teaspoon sea salt

Directions:

1. Insert the Grill Grate and close the hood. Select GRILL, set the temperature to MAX, and set the time to 10 minutes. Select START/STOP to begin preheating.
2. In a large bowl, toss the carrots and oil until well coated.
3. When the unit beeps to signify it has preheated, place carrots on the center of the Grill Grate. Close the hood and GRILL for 5 minutes.
4. Meanwhile, in a small bowl, whisk together the butter, brown sugar, honey, and salt.
5. After 5 minutes, open the hood and baste the carrots with the glaze. Using tongs, turn the carrots and baste the other side. Close the hood and GRILL for another 5 minutes.
6. When cooking is complete, serve immediately.

Cheesy Steak Fries

Servings: 5
Cooking Time: 20 Minutes

Ingredients:

- 1 bag frozen steak fries
- Cooking spray
- Salt and pepper, to taste
- ½ cup beef gravy
- 1 cup shredded Mozzarella cheese
- 2 scallions, green parts only, chopped

Directions:

1. Insert the Crisper Basket and close the hood. Select AIR CRISP, set the temperature to 400°F, and set the time to 20 minutes. Select START/STOP to begin preheating.
2. Place the frozen steak fries in the basket. Close the hood and AIR CRISP for 10 minutes. Shake the basket and spritz the fries with cooking spray. Sprinkle with salt and pepper. AIR CRISP for an additional 8 minutes.
3. Pour the beef gravy into a medium, microwave-safe bowl. Microwave for 30 seconds, or until the gravy is warm.
4. Sprinkle the fries with the cheese. Close the hood and AIR CRISP for an additional 2 minutes, until the cheese is melted.
5. Transfer the fries to a serving dish. Drizzle the fries with gravy and sprinkle the scallions on top for a green garnish. Serve.

Avocado Egg Rolls

Servings: 4
Cooking Time: 10 Minutes

Ingredients:

- 4 avocados, pitted and diced
- ½ white onion, diced
- ⅓ cup sun-dried tomatoes, chopped
- 1 (16-ounce) package egg roll wrappers (about 20 wrappers)
- ¼ cup water, for sealing
- 4 tablespoons avocado oil

Directions:

1. Insert the Grill Grate and close the hood. Select GRILL, set the temperature to LO, and set the time to 10 minutes. Select START/STOP to begin preheating.
2. While the unit is preheating, place the diced avocado in a large bowl. Add the onion and sun-dried tomatoes and gently fold together, being careful to not mash the avocado.
3. Place an egg roll wrapper on a flat surface with a corner facing you (like a diamond). Add 2 to 3 tablespoons of the filling in the center of the wrapper. The amount should be about 2½ inches wide. Gently lift the bottom corner of the wrapper over the filling, fold in the sides, and roll away from you to close. Dip your finger into the water and run it over the top corner of the wrapper to seal it. Continue filling, folding, and sealing the rest of the egg rolls.
4. When the unit beeps to signify it has preheated, brush the avocado oil on all sides of the egg rolls. Place the egg rolls on the Grill Grate, seam-side down. Close the hood and grill for 5 minutes.
5. After 5 minutes, open the hood and flip the egg rolls. Give them another brush of avocado oil. Close the hood and cook for 5 minutes more.
6. When cooking is complete, the wrappers will be golden brown. Remove from the grill and serve.

Balsamic Broccoli

Servings: 4
Cooking Time: 10 Minutes

Ingredients:

- 4 tablespoons soy sauce
- 4 tablespoons balsamic vinegar
- 2 tablespoons canola oil
- 2 teaspoons maple syrup
- 2 heads broccoli, trimmed into florets
- Red pepper flakes, for garnish
- Sesame seeds, for garnish

Directions:

1. Insert the Grill Grate and close the hood. Select GRILL, set the temperature to MAX, and set the time to 10 minutes. Select START/STOP to begin preheating.
2. While the unit is preheating, in a large bowl, whisk together the soy sauce, balsamic vinegar, oil, and maple syrup. Add the broccoli and toss to coat evenly.
3. When the unit beeps to signify it has preheated, place the broccoli on the Grill Grate. Close the hood and GRILL for 8 to 10 minutes, until charred on all sides.
4. When cooking is complete, place the broccoli on a large serving platter. Garnish with red pepper flakes and sesame seeds. Serve immediately.

Deluxe Cheese Sandwiches

Servings: 4 To 8
Cooking Time: 5 To 6 Minutes

Ingredients:

- 8 ounces Brie
- 8 slices oat nut bread
- 1 large ripe pear, cored and cut into ½-inch-thick slices
- 2 tablespoons butter, melted

Directions:

1. Select BAKE, set the temperature to 360°F, and set the time to 6 minutes. Select START/STOP to begin preheating. .
2. Make the sandwiches: Spread each of 4 slices of bread with ¼ of the Brie. Top the Brie with the pear slices and remaining 4 bread slices.
3. Brush the melted butter lightly on both sides of each sandwich.
4. Arrange the sandwiches in a baking pan. You may need to work in batches to avoid overcrowding.
5. Place the pan directly in the pot. Close the hood and BAKE for 5 to 6 minutes until the cheese is melted. Repeat with the remaining sandwiches.
6. Serve warm.

Seafood Recipes

Mom's Lemon-pepper Salmon

Servings: 4
Cooking Time: 8 Minutes

Ingredients:

- ¼ cup mayonnaise
- 4 (4- to 5-ounce) skin-on salmon fillets
- 1 tablespoon lemon-pepper seasoning

Directions:

1. Insert the Grill Grate and close the hood. Select GRILL, set the temperature to MED, and set the time to 8 minutes. Select START/STOP to begin preheating.
2. While the unit is preheating, spread the mayonnaise evenly on the flesh of each salmon fillet. Season with the lemon pepper.
3. When the unit beeps to signify it has preheated, place the fillets on the Grill Grate, skin-side down. Close the hood and cook for 8 minutes.
4. When cooking is complete, the salmon will be opaque and should flake easily with a fork. (If you want, you can also use the Smart Thermometer at the end of cooking to check that the internal temperature of the salmon has reached 145°F.) Remove the salmon from the grill and serve.

Buttered Lobster Tails

Servings: 6
Cooking Time: 7 Minutes
Ingredients:

- 6 (4-ounce) lobster tails
- Paprika
- Salt
- Freshly ground black pepper
- 4 tablespoons (½ stick) unsalted butter, melted
- 3 garlic cloves, minced

Directions:

1. Place the lobster tails shell-side up on a cutting board. Using kitchen shears, cut each shell down the center, stopping at the base of the tail. Carefully crack open the shell by sliding your thumbs between the shell and meat and delicately pulling apart. Wiggle, pull, and lift the meat out of the shell. Remove the vein and digestive tract, if present. Rest the meat on top of the shell for a beautiful display.
2. Insert the Grill Grate and close the hood. Select GRILL, set the temperature to HI, and set the time to 7 minutes. Select START/STOP to begin preheating.
3. While the unit is preheating, season the lobster meat with paprika, salt, and pepper.
4. In a small bowl, combine the melted butter and garlic.
5. When the unit beeps to signify it has preheated, place the lobster tails on their shells on the Grill Grate. Close the hood and grill for 4 minutes.
6. After 4 minutes, open the hood and brush the garlic butter on the lobster meat. Close the hood and cook for 3 minutes more.
7. When cooking is complete, the lobster meat will be opaque and the shell will be orangey red. Serve with more melted butter or a sauce of your choice.

Crusted Codfish

Servings: 4
Cooking Time: 8 Minutes
Ingredients:

- 1 cup panko bread crumbs
- 2 tablespoons grated Parmesan cheese
- ¼ cup chopped pistachios
- 4 (4-ounce) frozen cod fillets, thawed
- 4 tablespoons Dijon mustard
- Cooking spray

Directions:

1. Insert the Grill Grate and close the hood. Select GRILL, set the temperature to HI, and set the time to 8 minutes. Select START/STOP to begin preheating.
2. While the unit is preheating, on a large plate, mix together the panko bread crumbs, Parmesan cheese, and pistachios. Evenly coat both sides of the cod fillets with the mustard, then press the fillets on the panko mixture on both sides to create a crust.
3. When the unit beeps to signify it has preheated, spray the crusted fillets with cooking spray and place them on the Grill Grate. Close the hood and grill for 4 minutes.
4. After 4 minutes, open the hood and flip the fillets. Close the hood and cook for 4 minutes more.
5. When cooking is complete, remove the fillets from the grill and serve.

Shrimp Boil

Servings: 6
Cooking Time: 10 Minutes

Ingredients:

- 2 tablespoons lemon-pepper seasoning
- 2 tablespoons light brown sugar, packed
- 2 tablespoons minced garlic
- 2 tablespoons Old Bay seasoning
- ¼ teaspoon Cajun seasoning
- ¼ teaspoon paprika
- ¼ teaspoon cayenne pepper
- 1 teaspoon garlic powder
- 1½ cups (3 sticks) unsalted butter, cut into quarters
- 2 pounds shrimp

Directions:

1. Insert the Cooking Pot and close the hood. Select GRILL, set the temperature to MED, and set the time to 10 minutes. Select START/STOP to begin preheating.
2. While the unit is preheating, in a small bowl, combine the lemon pepper, brown sugar, minced garlic, Old Bay seasoning, Cajun seasoning, paprika, cayenne pepper, and garlic powder.
3. When the unit beeps to signify it has preheated, place the butter and the lemon-pepper mixture in the Cooking Pot. Insert the Grill Grate and place the shrimp on it in a single layer. Close the hood and grill for 5 minutes.
4. After 5 minutes, open the hood and use grill mitts to remove the Grill Grate. Place the shrimp in the Cooking Pot. Stir to combine. Close the hood and cook for 5 minutes more.
5. When cooking is complete, open the hood and stir once more. Then close the hood and let the butter set with the shrimp for 5 minutes. Serve.

Tilapia With Cilantro And Ginger

Servings: 4
Cooking Time: 8 Minutes

Ingredients:

- Extra-virgin olive oil
- 4 (8-ounce) tilapia fillets
- 2 tablespoons soy sauce
- 1 teaspoon sesame oil
- 1 tablespoon honey
- 1 tablespoon peeled minced fresh ginger
- ½ cup chopped fresh cilantro

Directions:

1. Insert the Cooking Pot and close the hood. Select GRILL, set the temperature to HI, and set the time to 8 minutes. Select START/STOP to begin preheating.
2. While the unit is preheating, drizzle the fish fillets with olive oil.
3. When the unit beeps to signify it has preheated, place the fillets in the Cooking Pot in a single layer. Close the hood and cook for 6 minutes.
4. While the fish is cooking, in a small bowl, whisk together the soy sauce, sesame oil, honey, ginger, and cilantro.
5. After 6 minutes, open the hood and pour the sauce over the fillets. Close the hood and cook for 2 minutes more.
6. When cooking is complete, remove the fillets from the grill and serve.

Coconut Shrimp With Orange Chili Sauce

Servings:44
Cooking Time: 16 Minutes
Ingredients:
- For the coconut shrimp
- 2 large eggs
- 1 cup sweetened coconut flakes
- 1 cup panko bread crumbs
- ½ teaspoon salt
- ¼ teaspoon freshly ground black pepper
- 2 pounds jumbo shrimp, peeled
- For the orange chili sauce
- ½ cup orange marmalade
- 1 teaspoon sriracha or ¼ teaspoon red pepper flakes

Directions:
1.   Insert the Grill Grate and close the hood. Select GRILL, set the temperature to HI, and set the time to 16 minutes. Select START/STOP to begin preheating.
2.   While the unit is preheating, create an assembly line with 2 large bowls. In one bowl, whisk the eggs. In the other bowl, combine the coconut flakes, panko bread crumbs, salt, and pepper. One at a time, dip the shrimp in the egg and then into the coconut flakes until fully coated.
3.   When the unit beeps to signify it has preheated, place half the shrimp on the Grill Grate in a single layer. Close the hood and cook for 4 minutes.
4.   After 4 minutes, open the hood and flip the shrimp. Close the hood and cook for 4 minutes more. After 4 minutes, open the hood and remove the shrimp from the grill.
5.   Repeat steps 3 and 4 for the remaining shrimp.
6.   To make the orange chili sauce
7.   In a small bowl, combine the orange marmalade and sriracha. Serve as a dipping sauce alongside the coconut shrimp.

Tomato-stuffed Grilled Sole

Servings: 6
Cooking Time: 7 Minutes
Ingredients:
- 6 tablespoons mayonnaise
- 1 teaspoon garlic powder
- 1 (14-ounce) can diced tomatoes, drained
- 6 (4-ounce) sole fillets
- Cooking spray
- 6 tablespoons panko bread crumbs

Directions:
1.   Insert the Grill Grate and close the hood. Select GRILL, set the temperature to HI, and set the time to 7 minutes. Select START/STOP to begin preheating.
2.   While the unit is preheating, in a small bowl, combine the mayonnaise and garlic powder. Slowly fold in the tomatoes, making sure to be gentle so they don't turn to mush. Place the sole fillets on a large, flat surface and spread the mayonnaise across the top of each. Roll up the fillets, creating pinwheels. Spray the top of each roll with cooking spray, then press 1 tablespoon of panko bread crumbs on top of each.
3.   When the unit beeps to signify it has preheated, place the fillets on the Grill Grate, seam-side down. Close the hood and grill for 7 minutes.
4.   When cooking is complete, the panko bread crumbs will be crisp, and the fish will have turned opaque. Remove the fish from the grill and serve.

Garlic Butter Shrimp Kebabs

Servings: 4
Cooking Time: 10 Minutes
Ingredients:
- 2 tablespoons unsalted butter, at room temperature
- 4 garlic cloves, minced
- 2 pounds jumbo shrimp, peeled
- 1 tablespoon garlic salt
- 1 teaspoon dried parsley

Directions:
1.   Insert the Grill Grate. Place the butter and minced garlic in a heat-safe bowl, place the bowl on the Grill Grate, and close the hood. Select GRILL, set the temperature to HI, and set the time to 5 minutes. Select START/STOP to begin preheating. After 1 minute of preheating (set a separate timer), remove the bowl with the butter. Close the hood to continue preheating.
2.   While the unit is preheating, place 4 or 5 shrimp on each of 8 skewers, with at least 1 inch left at the bottom. Place the skewers on a large plate. Lightly coat them with the garlic salt and parsley.
3.   When the unit beeps to signify it has preheated, place 4 skewers on the Grill Grate. Brush some of the melted garlic butter on the shrimp. Close the hood and grill for 2 minutes, 30 seconds.
4.   After 2 minutes, 30 seconds, open the hood and brush the shrimp with garlic butter again, then flip the skewers. Brush on more garlic butter. Close the hood and cook for 2 minutes, 30 seconds more.
5.   When cooking is complete, the shrimp will be opaque and pink. Remove the skewers from the grill. Select GRILL, set the temperature to HI, and set the time to 5 minutes. Select START/STOP to begin and press PREHEAT to skip preheating. Repeat steps 3 and 4 for the remaining skewers. When all the skewers are cooked, serve.

Honey-walnut Shrimp

Servings: 4
Cooking Time: 8 Minutes
Ingredients:
- 2 ounces walnuts
- 2 tablespoons honey
- 1 egg
- 1 cup panko bread crumbs
- 1 pound shrimp, peeled
- ½ cup mayonnaise
- 1 teaspoon powdered sugar
- 2 tablespoons heavy (whipping) cream
- Scallions, both white and green parts, sliced, for garnish

Directions:
1.   Insert the Grill Grate. In a small heat-safe bowl, combine the walnuts and honey, then place the bowl on the Grill Grate and close the hood. Select GRILL, set the temperature to HI, and set the time to 8 minutes. Select START/STOP to begin preheating. After 2 minutes of preheating (set a separate timer), remove the bowl. Close the hood to continue preheating.
2.   While the unit is preheating, create an assembly line with 2 large bowls. In the first bowl, whisk the egg. Put the panko bread crumbs in the other bowl. One at a time, dip the shrimp in the egg and then into the panko bread crumbs until well coated. Place the breaded shrimp on a plate.
3.   When the unit beeps to signify it has preheated, place the shrimp on the Grill Grate in a single layer. Close the hood and cook for 4 minutes.
4.   After 4 minutes, open the hood and flip the shrimp. Close the hood and cook for 4 minutes more.
5.   While the shrimp are cooking, in a large bowl, combine the mayonnaise, powdered sugar, and heavy cream and mix until the sugar has dissolved.
6.   When cooking is complete, remove the shrimp from the grill. Add the cooked shrimp and honey walnuts to the mayonnaise mixture and gently fold them together. Garnish with scallions and serve.

Desserts Recipes

Apple Pie Crumble

Servings: 4
Cooking Time: 20 Minutes
Ingredients:

- 3 small apples, such as Honeycrisp, Gala, Pink Lady, or Granny Smith, peeled, cored, and cut into ⅛-inch-thick slices
- ¼ cup granulated sugar
- ½ teaspoon cinnamon
- ½ cup quick-cooking oatmeal
- 4 tablespoons (½ stick) unsalted butter, at room temperature
- ½ cup all-purpose flour
- ½ cup light brown sugar, packed

Directions:

1. Insert the Cooking Pot and close the hood. Select GRILL, set the temperature to LO, and set the time to 20 minutes. Select START/STOP to begin preheating.
2. While the unit is preheating, put the apples in a large bowl and coat with the granulated sugar and cinnamon. In a medium bowl, combine the oatmeal, butter, flour, and brown sugar, stirring to make clumps for the top layer.
3. Place the apples in a 6-inch springform pan in an even layer. Spread the oatmeal topping over the apples.
4. When the unit beeps to signify it has preheated, place the pan in the Cooking Pot. Close the hood and cook for 20 minutes.
5. After 20 minutes, open the hood and remove the pan from the unit. The apples should be soft and the topping golden brown. Serve.

Peanut Butter-chocolate Bread Pudding

Servings: 8
Cooking Time: 10 To 12 Minutes
Ingredients:

- 1 egg
- 1 egg yolk
- ¾ cup chocolate milk
- 3 tablespoons brown sugar
- 3 tablespoons peanut butter
- 2 tablespoons cocoa powder
- 1 teaspoon vanilla
- 5 slices firm white bread, cubed
- Nonstick cooking spray

Directions:

1. Select BAKE, set the temperature to 330°F, and set the time to 12 minutes. Select START/STOP to begin preheating.
2. Spritz a baking pan with nonstick cooking spray.
3. Whisk together the egg, egg yolk, chocolate milk, brown sugar, peanut butter, cocoa powder, and vanilla until well combined.
4. Fold in the bread cubes and stir to mix well. Allow the bread soak for 10 minutes.
5. When ready, transfer the egg mixture to the prepared baking pan.
6. Place the pan directly in the pot. Close the hood and BAKE for 10 to 12 minutes, or until the pudding is just firm to the touch.
7. Serve at room temperature.

Banana And Walnut Cake

Servings: 6

Cooking Time: 25 Minutes

Ingredients:

- 1 pound bananas, mashed
- 8 ounces flour
- 6 ounces sugar
- 3.5 ounces walnuts, chopped
- 2.5 ounces butter, melted
- 2 eggs, lightly beaten
- ¼ teaspoon baking soda

Directions:

1. Select BAKE, set the temperature to 355°F, and set the time to 10 minutes. Select START/STOP to begin preheating.

2. In a bowl, combine the sugar, butter, egg, flour, and baking soda with a whisk. Stir in the bananas and walnuts.

3. Transfer the mixture to a greased baking pan. Place the pan directly in the pot. Close the hood and BAKE for 10 minutes.

4. Reduce the temperature to 330°F and bake for another 15 minutes. Serve hot.

Grilled Apple Fries With Caramel Cream Cheese Dip

Servings: 4

Cooking Time: 5 Minutes

Ingredients:

- 4 apples, such as Honeycrisp, Gala, Pink Lady, or Granny Smith, peeled, cored, and sliced
- ¼ cup heavy (whipping) cream
- 1 tablespoon granulated sugar
- ¼ teaspoon cinnamon
- ¼ cup all-purpose flour
- 4 ounces cream cheese, at room temperature
- 1 tablespoon caramel sauce
- 1 tablespoon light brown sugar, packed

Directions:

1. Insert the Grill Grate and close the hood. Select GRILL, set the temperature to MAX, and set the time to 5 minutes. Select START/STOP to begin preheating.

2. In a large bowl, toss the apple slices with the heavy cream, granulated sugar, and cinnamon to coat. Slowly shake in the flour and continue mixing to coat.

3. In a small bowl, mix together the cream cheese, caramel sauce, and brown sugar until smooth. Set aside.

4. When the unit beeps to signify it has preheated, place the apples on the Grill Grate in a single layer. Close the hood and grill for 2 minutes, 30 seconds.

5. After 2 minutes, 30 seconds, open the hood and flip and toss the apples around. Close the hood and cook for 2 minutes, 30 seconds more.

6. When cooking is complete, open the hood and remove the apple chips from the grill. Serve with the sauce.

Curry Peaches, Pears, And Plums

Servings: 6 To 8

Cooking Time: 5 Minutes

Ingredients:

- 2 peaches
- 2 firm pears
- 2 plums
- 2 tablespoons melted butter
- 1 tablespoon honey
- 2 to 3 teaspoons curry powder

Directions:

1. Insert the Crisper Basket and close the hood. Select BAKE, set the temperature to 325°F, and set the time to 8 minutes. Select START/STOP to begin preheating.

2. Cut the peaches in half, remove the pits, and cut each half in half again. Cut the pears in half, core them, and remove the stem. Cut each half in half again. Do the same with the plums.

3. Spread a large sheet of heavy-duty foil on the work surface. Arrange the fruit on the foil and drizzle with the butter and honey. Sprinkle with the curry powder.

4. Wrap the fruit in the foil, making sure to leave some air space in the packet.

5. Put the foil package in the basket. Close the hood and BAKE for 5 to 8 minutes, shaking the basket once during the cooking time, until the fruit is soft.

6. Serve immediately.

Mixed Berry And Cream Cheese Puff Pastries

Servings: 4

Cooking Time: 8 Minutes

Ingredients:

- 1 sheet puff pastry (thawed if frozen)
- 4 tablespoons (½ stick) unsalted butter, melted
- 6 ounces cream cheese, at room temperature
- 1 cup mixed-berry jam

Directions:

1. Insert the Grill Grate and close the hood. Select GRILL, set the temperature to LO, and set the time to 8 minutes. Select START/STOP to begin preheating.

2. While the unit is preheating, unfold the pastry dough on a flat surface. Cut the dough into four equal-size pieces. Brush each piece with the butter. Fold in ¼ to ½ inch of each side of each piece of dough to create a pocket for the filling. Spread a layer of the cream cheese across each pastry pocket and then add ¼ cup of jam on top of each.

3. When the unit beeps to signify it has preheated, place the pastries on the Grill Grate. Close the hood and grill for 8 minutes.

4. When cooking is complete, the puff pastry will be golden brown and the cream cheese and jam may be infused and melted together. Remove the pastries from the grill and serve.

Orange Cake

Servings: 8

Cooking Time: 23 Minutes

Ingredients:

- Nonstick baking spray with flour
- 1¼ cups all-purpose flour
- ⅓ cup yellow cornmeal
- ¾ cup white sugar
- 1 teaspoon baking soda
- ¼ cup safflower oil
- 1¼ cups orange juice, divided
- 1 teaspoon vanilla
- ¼ cup powdered sugar

Directions:

1. Select BAKE, set the temperature to 350°F, and set the time to 23 minutes. Select START/STOP to begin preheating.
2. Spray a baking pan with nonstick spray and set aside.
3. In a medium bowl, combine the flour, cornmeal, sugar, baking soda, safflower oil, 1 cup of the orange juice, and vanilla, and mix well.
4. Pour the batter into the baking pan. Place the pan directly in the pot. Close the hood and BAKE for 23 minutes or until a toothpick inserted in the center of the cake comes out clean.
5. Remove the cake from the grill and place on a cooling rack. Using a toothpick, make about 20 holes in the cake.
6. In a small bowl, combine remaining ¼ cup of orange juice and the powdered sugar and stir well. Drizzle this mixture over the hot cake slowly so the cake absorbs it.
7. Cool completely, then cut into wedges to serve.

Rum Grilled Pineapple Sundaes

Servings: 6

Cooking Time: 8 Minutes

Ingredients:

- ½ cup dark rum
- ½ cup packed brown sugar
- 1 teaspoon ground cinnamon, plus more for garnish
- 1 pineapple, cored and sliced
- Vanilla ice cream, for serving

Directions:

1. In a large shallow bowl or storage container, combine the rum, sugar, and cinnamon. Add the pineapple slices and arrange them in a single layer. Coat with the mixture, then let soak for at least 5 minutes per side.
2. Insert the Grill Grate and close the hood. Select GRILL, set the temperature to MAX, and set the time to 8 minutes. Select START/STOP to begin preheating.
3. While the unit is preheating, strain the extra rum sauce from the pineapple.
4. When the unit beeps to signify it has preheated, place the fruit on the Grill Grate in a single layer (you may need to do this in multiple batches). Gently press the fruit down to maximize grill marks. Close the hood and GRILL for about 6 to 8 minutes without flipping. If working in batches, remove the pineapple, and repeat this step for the remaining pineapple slices.
5. When cooking is complete, remove, and top each pineapple ring with a scoop of ice cream. Sprinkle with cinnamon and serve immediately.

Coffee Chocolate Cake

Servings: 8
Cooking Time: 30 Minutes
Ingredients:
- Dry Ingredients:
- 1½ cups almond flour
- ½ cup coconut meal
- ⅔ cup Swerve
- 1 teaspoon baking powder
- ¼ teaspoon salt
- Wet Ingredients:
- 1 egg
- 1 stick butter, melted
- ½ cup hot strongly brewed coffee
- Topping:
- ½ cup confectioner's Swerve
- ¼ cup coconut flour
- 3 tablespoons coconut oil
- 1 teaspoon ground cinnamon
- ½ teaspoon ground cardamom

Directions:
1. Select BAKE, set the temperature to 330°F, and set the time to 30 minutes. Select START/STOP to begin preheating.
2. In a medium bowl, combine the almond flour, coconut meal, Swerve, baking powder, and salt.
3. In a large bowl, whisk the egg, melted butter, and coffee until smooth.
4. Add the dry mixture to the wet and stir until well incorporated. Transfer the batter to a greased baking pan.
5. Stir together all the ingredients for the topping in a small bowl. Spread the topping over the batter and smooth the top with a spatula.
6. Place the pan directly in the pot. Close the hood and BAKE for 30 minutes, or until the cake springs back when gently pressed with your fingers.
7. Rest for 10 minutes before serving.

Chocolate S'mores

Servings: 12
Cooking Time: 3 Minutes
Ingredients:
- 12 whole cinnamon graham crackers
- 2 chocolate bars, broken into 12 pieces
- 12 marshmallows

Directions:
1. Insert the Crisper Basket and close the hood. Select BAKE, set the temperature to 350°F, and set the time to 3 minutes. Select START/STOP to begin preheating.
2. Halve each graham cracker into 2 squares.
3. Put 6 graham cracker squares in the basket. Do not stack. Put a piece of chocolate into each. Close the hood and BAKE for 2 minutes.
4. Open the grill and add a marshmallow onto each piece of melted chocolate. Bake for 1 additional minute.
5. Remove the cooked s'mores from the grill, then repeat steps 2 and 3 for the remaining 6 s'mores.
6. Top with the remaining graham cracker squares and serve.

Orange Coconut Cake

Servings: 6
Cooking Time: 17 Minutes
Ingredients:

- 1 stick butter, melted
- ¾ cup granulated Swerve
- 2 eggs, beaten
- ¾ cup coconut flour
- ¼ teaspoon salt
- ⅓ teaspoon grated nutmeg
- ⅓ cup coconut milk
- 1¼ cups almond flour
- ½ teaspoon baking powder
- 2 tablespoons unsweetened orange jam
- Cooking spray

Directions:

1. Select BAKE, set the temperature to 355°F, and set the time to 17 minutes. Select START/STOP to begin preheating.
2. Coat a baking pan with cooking spray. Set aside.
3. In a large mixing bowl, whisk together the melted butter and granulated Swerve until fluffy.
4. Mix in the beaten eggs and whisk again until smooth. Stir in the coconut flour, salt, and nutmeg and gradually pour in the coconut milk. Add the remaining ingredients and stir until well incorporated.
5. Scrape the batter into the baking pan.
6. Place the pan directly in the pot. Close the hood and BAKE for 17 minutes until the top of the cake springs back when gently pressed with your fingers.
7. Remove from the grill to a wire rack to cool. Serve chilled.

Grilled Banana S'mores

Servings: 4
Cooking Time: 6 Minutes
Ingredients:

- 4 large bananas
- 1 cup milk chocolate chips
- 1 cup mini marshmallows
- 4 graham crackers, crushed

Directions:

1. Insert the Cooking Pot and close the hood. Select GRILL, set the temperature to HI, and set the time to 6 minutes. Select START/STOP to begin preheating.
2. While the unit is preheating, prepare the banana boats. Starting at the bottom of a banana, slice the peel lengthwise up one side and then the opposite side. Pull the top half of the peel back, revealing the fruit underneath, but keeping the bottom of the banana peel intact. With a spoon, carefully scoop out some of the banana. (Eat it or set it aside.) Repeat with each banana. Equally divide the chocolate chips and marshmallows between the banana boats.
3. When the unit beeps to signify it has preheated, place the bananas in the Cooking Pot. Close the hood and cook for 6 minutes.
4. When cooking is complete, remove the bananas from the grill and sprinkle the crushed graham crackers on top. Serve.

Grilled Strawberry Pound Cake

Servings: 8
Cooking Time: 8 Minutes

Ingredients:

- 1 loaf pound cake, cut into ¼-inch-thick slices (8 slices)
- 4 tablespoons (½ stick) unsalted butter, melted
- 2 cups strawberries, sliced
- 1 tablespoon granulated sugar
- Juice of ¼ lemon

Directions:

1. Insert the Grill Grate and close the hood. Select GRILL, set the temperature to HI, and set the time to 8 minutes. Select START/STOP to begin preheating.

2. While the unit is preheating, brush both sides of the pound cake slices with the melted butter. In a small bowl, combine the strawberries, sugar, and lemon juice.

3. When the unit beeps to signify it has preheated, place 4 slices of pound cake on the Grill Grate. Close the hood and grill for 2 minutes.

4. After 2 minutes, open the hood and flip the pound cake slices. Top each with ¼ cup of strawberries. Close the hood and cook for 2 minutes.

5. After 2 minutes, open the hood and carefully remove the grilled pound cake. Repeat steps 3 and 4 with the remaining pound cake and strawberries. Serve.

Blackberry Chocolate Cake

Servings: 8
Cooking Time: 22 Minutes

Ingredients:

- ½ cup butter, at room temperature
- 2 ounces Swerve
- 4 eggs
- 1 cup almond flour
- 1 teaspoon baking soda
- ⅓ teaspoon baking powder
- ½ cup cocoa powder
- 1 teaspoon orange zest
- ⅓ cup fresh blackberries

Directions:

1. Select BAKE, set the temperature to 335°F, and set the time to 22 minutes. Select START/STOP to begin preheating.

2. With an electric mixer or hand mixer, beat the butter and Swerve until creamy.

3. One at a time, mix in the eggs and beat again until fluffy.

4. Add the almond flour, baking soda, baking powder, cocoa powder, orange zest and mix well. Add the butter mixture to the almond flour mixture and stir until well blended. Fold in the blackberries.

5. Scrape the batter to a baking pan. Place the pan directly in the pot. Close the hood and BAKE for 22 minutes. Check the cake for doneness: If a toothpick inserted into the center of the cake comes out clean, it's done.

6. Allow the cake cool on a wire rack to room temperature. Serve immediately.

Chocolate Molten Cake

Servings: 4
Cooking Time: 10 Minutes
Ingredients:

- 3.5 ounces butter, melted
- 3½ tablespoons sugar
- 3.5 ounces chocolate, melted
- 1½ tablespoons flour
- 2 eggs

Directions:

1. Select BAKE, set the temperature to 375°F, and set the time to 10 minutes. Select START/STOP to begin preheating.
2. Grease four ramekins with a little butter.
3. Rigorously combine the eggs, butter, and sugar before stirring in the melted chocolate.
4. Slowly fold in the flour.
5. Spoon an equal amount of the mixture into each ramekin.
6. Put them in the pot. Close the hood and BAKE for 10 minutes.
7. Put the ramekins upside-down on plates and let the cakes fall out. Serve hot.

Oatmeal And Carrot Cookie Cups

Servings:16
Cooking Time: 8 Minutes
Ingredients:

- 3 tablespoons unsalted butter, at room temperature
- ¼ cup packed brown sugar
- 1 tablespoon honey
- 1 egg white
- ½ teaspoon vanilla extract
- ⅓ cup finely grated carrot
- ½ cup quick-cooking oatmeal
- ⅓ cup whole-wheat pastry flour
- ½ teaspoon baking soda
- ¼ cup dried cherries

Directions:

1. Select BAKE, set the temperature to 350°F, and set the time to 8 minutes. Select START/STOP to begin preheating.
2. In a medium bowl, beat the butter, brown sugar, and honey until well combined.
3. Add the egg white, vanilla, and carrot. Beat to combine.
4. Stir in the oatmeal, pastry flour, and baking soda.
5. Stir in the dried cherries.
6. Double up 32 mini muffin foil cups to make 16 cups. Fill each with about 4 teaspoons of dough. Place the cookie cups directly in the pot.
7. Close the hood and BAKE for 8 minutes, 8 at a time, or until light golden brown and just set. Serve warm.

Lemony Blackberry Crisp

Servings: 1
Cooking Time: 20 Minutes
Ingredients:

- 2 tablespoons lemon juice
- ⅓ cup powdered erythritol
- ¼ teaspoon xantham gum
- 2 cup blackberries
- 1 cup crunchy granola

Directions:

1. Select BAKE, set the temperature to 350°F, and set the time to 15 minutes. Select START/STOP to begin preheating.
2. In a bowl, combine the lemon juice, erythritol, xantham gum, and blackberries. Transfer to a round baking pan and cover with aluminum foil.
3. Place the pan directly in the pot. Close the hood and BAKE for 12 minutes.
4. Take care when removing the pan from the grill. Give the blackberries a stir and top with the granola.
5. Return the pan to the grill and bake at 320°F for an additional 3 minutes. Serve once the granola has turned brown and enjoy.

Orange And Anise Cake

Servings: 6
Cooking Time: 20 Minutes
Ingredients:

- 1 stick butter, at room temperature
- 5 tablespoons liquid monk fruit
- 2 eggs plus 1 egg yolk, beaten
- ⅓ cup hazelnuts, roughly chopped
- 3 tablespoons sugar-free orange marmalade
- 6 ounces unbleached almond flour
- 1 teaspoon baking soda
- ½ teaspoon baking powder
- ½ teaspoon ground cinnamon
- ½ teaspoon ground allspice
- ½ ground anise seed
- Cooking spray

Directions:

1. Select BAKE, set the temperature to 310°F, and set the time to 20 minutes. Select START/STOP to begin preheating.
2. Lightly spritz a baking pan with cooking spray.
3. In a mixing bowl, whisk the butter and liquid monk fruit until the mixture is pale and smooth. Mix in the beaten eggs, hazelnuts, and marmalade and whisk again until well incorporated.
4. Add the almond flour, baking soda, baking powder, cinnamon, allspice, anise seed and stir to mix well.
5. Scrape the batter into the prepared baking pan. Place the pan directly in the pot. Close the hood and BAKE for 20 minutes, or until the top of the cake springs back when gently pressed with your fingers.
6. Transfer to a wire rack and let the cake cool to room temperature. Serve immediately.

Vanilla Scones

Servings:18
Cooking Time: 15 Minutes
Ingredients:
- For the scones
- 2 cups almond flour
- ¼ cup granulated sugar
- ¼ teaspoon salt
- 1 tablespoon baking powder
- 2 large eggs
- 1 teaspoon vanilla extract
- 4 tablespoons (½ stick) unsalted butter, melted
- 2 tablespoons heavy (whipping) cream
- For the icing
- 1 cup powdered sugar
- 2 tablespoons heavy (whipping) cream
- 1 tablespoon vanilla extract

Directions:

1. In a large bowl, combine the almond flour, granulated sugar, salt, and baking powder. In another large bowl, whisk the eggs, then whisk in the vanilla, butter, and heavy cream. Add the dry ingredients to the wet and mix just until a dough forms.

2. Insert the Cooking Pot and close the hood. Select BAKE, set the temperature to 325°F, and set the time to 15 minutes. Select START/STOP to begin preheating.

3. While the unit is preheating, divide the dough into 3 equal pieces. Shape each piece into a disc about 1 inch thick and 5 inches in diameter. Cut each into 6 wedges, like slicing a pizza.

4. When the unit beeps to signify it has preheated, place the scones in the Cooking Pot, spacing them apart so they don't bake together. Close the hood and cook for 15 minutes.

5. While the scones are baking, in a small bowl, combine the powdered sugar, heavy cream, and vanilla. Stir until smooth.

6. After 15 minutes, open the hood and remove the scones. They are done baking when they have turned a light golden brown. Place on a wire rack to cool to room temperature. Drizzle the icing over the scones, or pour a tablespoonful on the top of each scone for an even glaze.

Peaches-and-cake Skewers

Servings: 4
Cooking Time: 8 Minutes
Ingredients:
- 1 loaf pound cake, cut into 1-inch cubes
- 4 peaches, sliced
- ½ cup condensed milk

Directions:

1. Insert the Grill Grate and close the hood. Select GRILL, set the temperature to HI, and set the time to 8 minutes. Select START/STOP to begin preheating.

2. While the unit is preheating, alternate cake cubes and peach slices, 3 or 4 pieces of each, on each of 12 skewers. Using a basting brush, brush the condensed milk onto the cake and peaches and place the skewers on a plate or baking sheet.

3. When the unit beeps to signify it has preheated, place 6 skewers on the Grill Grate. Close the hood and cook for 2 minutes.

4. After 2 minutes, open the hood and flip the skewers. Close the hood to cook for 2 minutes more.

5. After 2 minutes, open the hood and remove the skewers. Repeat steps 3 and 4 with the remaining 6 skewers. Serve.

Graham Cracker Cheesecake

Servings: 8
Cooking Time: 20 Minutes

Ingredients:

- 1 cup graham cracker crumbs
- 3 tablespoons softened butter
- 1½ packages cream cheese, softened
- ⅓ cup sugar
- 2 eggs
- 1 tablespoon flour
- 1 teaspoon vanilla
- ¼ cup chocolate syrup

Directions:

1. For the crust, combine the graham cracker crumbs and butter in a small bowl and mix well. Press into the bottom of a baking pan and put in the freezer to set.
2. For the filling, combine the cream cheese and sugar in a medium bowl and mix well. Beat in the eggs, one at a time. Add the flour and vanilla.
3. Select BAKE, set the temperature to 450°F, and set the time to 20 minutes. Select START/STOP to begin preheating.
4. Remove ⅔ cup of the filling to a small bowl and stir in the chocolate syrup until combined.
5. Pour the vanilla filling into the pan with the crust. Drop the chocolate filling over the vanilla filling by the spoonful. With a clean butter knife, stir the fillings in a zigzag pattern to marbleize them.
6. Place the pan directly in the pot. Close the hood and BAKE for 20 minutes or until the cheesecake is just set.
7. Cool on a wire rack for 1 hour, then chill in the refrigerator until the cheesecake is firm.
8. Serve immediately.

Ultimate Coconut Chocolate Cake

Servings: 10
Cooking Time: 15 Minutes

Ingredients:

- 1¼ cups unsweetened bakers' chocolate
- 1 stick butter
- 1 teaspoon liquid stevia
- ⅓ cup shredded coconut
- 2 tablespoons coconut milk
- 2 eggs, beaten
- Cooking spray

Directions:

1. Select BAKE, set the temperature to 330°F, and set the time to 15 minutes. Select START/STOP to begin preheating.
2. Lightly spritz a baking pan with cooking spray.
3. Place the chocolate, butter, and stevia in a microwave-safe bowl. Microwave for about 30 seconds until melted. Let the chocolate mixture cool to room temperature.
4. Add the remaining ingredients to the chocolate mixture and stir until well incorporated. Pour the batter into the prepared baking pan.
5. Place the pan directly in the pot. Close the hood and BAKE for 15 minutes, or until a toothpick inserted in the center comes out clean.
6. Remove from the pan and allow to cool for about 10 minutes before serving.

Pound Cake With Mixed Berries

Servings: 6
Cooking Time: 8 Minutes
Ingredients:

- 3 tablespoons unsalted butter, at room temperature
- 6 slices pound cake, sliced about 1-inch thick
- 1 cup fresh raspberries
- 1 cup fresh blueberries
- 3 tablespoons sugar
- ½ tablespoon fresh mint, minced

Directions:

1. Insert the Grill Grate and close the hood. Select GRILL, set the temperature to MAX, and set the time to 8 minutes. Select START/STOP to begin preheating.
2. While the unit is preheating, evenly spread the butter on both sides of each slice of pound cake.
3. When the unit beeps to signify it has preheated, place the pound cake on the Grill Grate. Close the hood and GRILL for 2 minutes.
4. After 2 minutes, flip the pound cake and GRILL for 2 minutes more, until golden brown. Repeat steps 3 and 4 for all of the pound cake slices.
5. While the pound cake grills, in a medium mixing bowl, combine the raspberries, blueberries, sugar, and mint.
6. When cooking is complete, plate the cake slices and serve topped with the berry mixture.

Black And White Brownies

Servings:1
Cooking Time: 20 Minutes
Ingredients:

- 1 egg
- ¼ cup brown sugar
- 2 tablespoons white sugar
- 2 tablespoons safflower oil
- 1 teaspoon vanilla
- ⅓ cup all-purpose flour
- ¼ cup cocoa powder
- ¼ cup white chocolate chips
- Nonstick cooking spray

Directions:

1. Select BAKE, set the temperature to 340°F, and set the time to 20 minutes. Select START/STOP to begin preheating.
2. Spritz a baking pan with nonstick cooking spray.
3. Whisk together the egg, brown sugar, and white sugar in a medium bowl. Mix in the safflower oil and vanilla and stir to combine.
4. Add the flour and cocoa powder and stir just until incorporated. Fold in the white chocolate chips.
5. Scrape the batter into the prepared baking pan.
6. Place the pan directly in the pot. Close the hood and BAKE for 20 minutes, or until the brownie springs back when touched lightly with your fingers.
7. Transfer to a wire rack and let cool for 30 minutes before slicing to serve.

Pecan Pie

Servings: 4
Cooking Time: 20 Minutes
Ingredients:

- 6 ounces cream cheese, at room temperature
- 4 tablespoons (½ stick) unsalted butter
- 2 large eggs
- 1 teaspoon vanilla extract
- 1 cup light brown sugar, packed
- 1 cup all-purpose flour
- ½ cup pecan halves

Directions:

1. Place the cream cheese and butter in a 7-inch silicone cake pan. Insert the Cooking Pot, place the cake pan in the pot, and close the hood. Select BAKE, set the temperature to 350°F, and set the time to 20 minutes. (If using a metal or glass cake pan, you may need to add 5 to 10 minutes to the baking time.) Select START/STOP to begin preheating. After 5 minutes of preheating (set a separate timer), open the hood and remove the cake pan. (The cream cheese and butter will be melted but not combined.) Close the hood to continue preheating.
2. While the unit is preheating, in a medium bowl, whisk together the eggs, vanilla, brown sugar, and 1½ tablespoons of the melted butter from the cake pan.
3. Transfer the remaining butter and cream cheese from the cake pan to a large bowl and mix to combine. (It may look a little like cottage cheese.) Slowly sift the flour into the bowl. Begin kneading and mixing the dough together with your hands. It may be sticky at first, but continue mixing until it forms into a smooth dough. Place the dough in the cake pan and press it into the bottom and up the sides of the pan to form a piecrust.
4. Pour the filling into the piecrust and top with the pecans.
5. When the unit beeps to signify it has preheated, place the cake pan in the Cooking Pot. Close the hood and bake for 20 minutes.
6. When cooking is complete, the crust edges will be golden brown. Remove the cake pan and let cool to room temperature before slicing and serving.

Fudge Pie

Servings: 8
Cooking Time: 25 To 30 Minutes
Ingredients:

- 1½ cups sugar
- ½ cup self-rising flour
- ⅓ cup unsweetened cocoa powder
- 3 large eggs, beaten
- 12 tablespoons butter, melted
- 1½ teaspoons vanilla extract
- 1 unbaked pie crust
- ¼ cup confectioners' sugar (optional)

Directions:

1. Select BAKE, set the temperature to 350°F, and set the time to 30 minutes. Select START/STOP to begin preheating.
2. Thoroughly combine the sugar, flour, and cocoa powder in a medium bowl. Add the beaten eggs and butter and whisk to combine. Stir in the vanilla.
3. Pour the prepared filling into the pie crust and transfer to the pot.
4. Close the hood and BAKE for 25 to 30 minutes until just set.
5. Allow the pie to cool for 5 minutes. Sprinkle with the confectioners' sugar, if desired. Serve warm.

Classic Pound Cake

Servings: 8
Cooking Time: 30 Minutes
Ingredients:

- 1 stick butter, at room temperature
- 1 cup Swerve
- 4 eggs
- 1½ cups coconut flour
- ½ cup buttermilk
- ½ teaspoon baking soda
- ½ teaspoon baking powder
- ¼ teaspoon salt
- 1 teaspoon vanilla essence
- A pinch of ground star anise
- A pinch of freshly grated nutmeg
- Cooking spray

Directions:

1. Select BAKE, set the temperature to 320°F, and set the time to 30 minutes. Select START/STOP to begin preheating.
2. Spray a baking pan with cooking spray.
3. With an electric mixer or hand mixer, beat the butter and Swerve until creamy. One at a time, mix in the eggs and whisk until fluffy. Add the remaining ingredients and stir to combine.
4. Transfer the batter to the prepared baking pan. Place the pan directly in the pot. Close the hood and BAKE for 30 minutes until the center of the cake is springy. Rotate the pan halfway through the cooking time.
5. Allow the cake to cool in the pan for 10 minutes before removing and serving.

Pumpkin Pudding

Servings: 4
Cooking Time: 15 Minutes
Ingredients:

- 3 cups pumpkin purée
- 3 tablespoons honey
- 1 tablespoon ginger
- 1 tablespoon cinnamon
- 1 teaspoon clove
- 1 teaspoon nutmeg
- 1 cup full-fat cream
- 2 eggs
- 1 cup sugar

Directions:

1. Select BAKE, set the temperature to 390°F, and set the time to 15 minutes. Select START/STOP to begin preheating.
2. In a bowl, stir all the ingredients together to combine.
3. Scrape the mixture into a greased baking pan. Place the pan directly in the pot. Close the hood and BAKE for 15 minutes.
4. Serve warm.

Simple Corn Biscuits

Servings: 6

Cooking Time: 15 Minutes

Ingredients:

- 1½ cups all-purpose flour, plus additional for dusting
- ½ cup yellow cornmeal
- 2½ teaspoons baking powder
- ½ teaspoon sea salt
- ⅓ cup vegetable shortening
- ⅔ cup buttermilk
- Nonstick cooking spray

Directions:

1. In a large bowl, combine the flour, cornmeal, baking powder, and salt.

2. Add the shortening, and cut it into the flour mixture, until well combined and the dough resembles a coarse meal. Add the buttermilk and stir together just until moistened.

3. Insert the Crisper Basket and close the hood. Select AIR CRISP, set the temperature to 350°F, and set the time to 15 minutes. Select START/STOP to begin preheating.

4. While the unit is preheating, dust a clean work surface with flour. Knead the mixture on the floured surface until a cohesive dough forms. Roll out the dough to an even thickness, then cut into biscuits with a 2-inch biscuit cutter.

5. When the unit beeps to signify it has preheated, coat the basket with cooking spray. Place 6 to 8 biscuits in the basket, well spaced, and spray each with cooking spray. Close the hood and AIR CRISP for 12 to 15 minutes, until golden brown.

6. Gently remove the biscuits from the basket, and place them on a wire rack to cool. Repeat with the remaining dough.

Biscuit Raisin Bread

Servings: 6 To 8

Cooking Time: 20 Minutes

Ingredients:

- 1 (12-ounce) package refrigerated buttermilk biscuits (10 biscuits)
- 8 ounces cream cheese, cut into 40 cubes
- ¼ cup light brown sugar, packed
- 4 tablespoons (½ stick) unsalted butter, melted
- ½ cup raisins

Directions:

1. Insert the Cooking Pot and close the hood. Select GRILL, set the temperature to LO, and set the time to 20 minutes. Select START/STOP to begin preheating.

2. While the unit is preheating, separate the biscuits and cut each into quarters. Flatten each quarter biscuit with your palm and place 1 cream cheese cube on the center. Wrap the dough around the cream cheese and press to seal, forming a ball. Place the biscuit balls in a 9-by-5-inch bread loaf pan. They will be layered over each other.

3. In a small bowl, combine the brown sugar and melted butter. Pour this over the biscuit balls evenly.

4. When the unit beeps to signify it has preheated, place the loaf pan in the Cooking Pot. Close the hood and grill for 10 minutes.

5. After 10 minutes, open the hood and evenly scatter the raisins on the top layer. Close the hood and cook for 10 minutes more.

6. When cooking is complete, remove the loaf pan from the pot. Remove the bread from the pan, slice, and serve.

Strawberry Pizza

Servings: 4
Cooking Time: 6 Minutes

Ingredients:

- 2 tablespoons all-purpose flour, plus more as needed
- ½ store-bought pizza dough
- 1 tablespoon canola oil
- 1 cup sliced fresh strawberries
- 1 tablespoon sugar
- ½ cup chocolate-hazelnut spread

Directions:

1. Insert the Grill Grate and close the hood. Select GRILL, set the temperature to MAX, and set the time to 6 minutes. Select START/STOP to begin preheating.

2. While the unit is preheating, dust a clean work surface with the flour. Place the dough on the floured surface, and roll it out to a 9-inch round of even thickness. Dust your rolling pin and work surface with additional flour, as needed, to ensure the dough does not stick.

3. Brush the surface of the rolled-out dough evenly with half the oil. Flip the dough over, and brush with the remaining oil. Poke the dough with a fork 5 or 6 times across its surface to prevent air pockets from forming during cooking.

4. When the unit beeps to signify it has preheated, place the dough on the Grill Grate. Close the hood and GRILL for 3 minutes.

5. After 3 minutes, flip the dough. Close the hood and continue grilling for the remaining 3 minutes.

6. Meanwhile, in a medium mixing bowl, combine the strawberries and sugar.

7. Transfer the pizza to a cutting board and let cool. Top with the chocolate-hazelnut spread and strawberries. Cut into pieces and serve.

RECIPES INDEX

A

Adobo Chicken 64

Apple And Walnut Muffins 23

Apple Pie Crumble 89

Arugula And Broccoli Salad 44

Asian-flavored Steak Kebabs 36

Asian-inspired Broccoli 49

Asparagus And Cheese Strata 17

Avocado Egg Rolls 83

Avocado Eggs 21

B

Bacon And Broccoli Bread Pudding 14

Bacon And Egg Stuffed Peppers 12

Bacon-wrapped Onion Rings And Spicy Aioli 77

Balsamic Broccoli 83

Balsamic Honey Mustard Lamb Chops 29

Balsamic Mushroom Sliders With Pesto 51

Banana And Walnut Cake 90

Banana Chips With Peanut Butter 19

Bean And Corn Stuffed Peppers 53

Beef And Scallion Rolls 37

Biscuit Raisin Bread 103

Black And White Brownies 100

Black Bean And Tomato Chili 48

Blackberry Chocolate Cake 95

Blackened Chicken 60

Blackened Chicken Breasts 56

Blt With Grilled Heirloom Tomato 74

Blueberry Dump Cake 15

Breaded Green Olives 80

Breakfast Chilaquiles 16

Breakfast Tater Tot Casserole 15

Brown-sugared Ham 29

Bruschetta With Tomato And Basil 81

Burnt Ends 34

Buttered Lobster Tails 85

Buttermilk Ranch Chicken Tenders 69

C

Candied Brussels Sprouts With Bacon 79

Caramelized Peaches 81

Cashew Pesto 72

Cayenne Sesame Nut Mix 74

Char Siew 32

Charred Green Beans With Sesame Seeds 42

Cheese And Spinach Stuffed Portobellos 42

Cheesy Apple Roll-ups 76

Cheesy Beef Meatballs 26

Cheesy Crab Toasts 77

Cheesy Macaroni Balls 52

Cheesy Steak Fries 82

Chermoula Beet Roast 47

Chicken Cordon Bleu Roll-ups 71

Chocolate Molten Cake 96

Chocolate S'mores 93

Cinnamon-spiced Acorn Squash 40

Citrus Carnitas 35

Classic Pound Cake 102

Coconut Shrimp With Orange Chili Sauce 87

Coffee Chocolate Cake 93

Cornflakes Toast Sticks 21

Crispy Chicken Strips 57

Crispy Dill Pickle Chicken Wings 67

Crispy Pork Belly Bites 34

Crusted Brussels Sprouts With Sage 41

Crusted Codfish 85

Crusted Pork Chops With Honey-maple Jalapeño Glaze 27

Crustless Broccoli Quiche 13

Cuban Sandwiches 80

Curry Peaches, Pears, And Plums 91

D

Deluxe Cheese Sandwiches 84

Dill Pickles 75

Double "egg" Plant (eggplant Omelets) 49

E

Easy Muffuletta Sliders With Olives 78

Egg And Avocado Burrito 18

Egg And Bacon Nests 23

Egg And Sausage Stuffed Breakfast Pockets 19

Everything Bagel Breakfast Bake 17

F

Fast Lamb Satay 25

Flatbread Pizza 41

Fried Buffalo Chicken Taquitos 68

Fried Potatoes With Peppers And Onions 18

Fudge Pie 101

G

Garlic Brown-butter Chicken With Tomatoes 59

Garlic Butter Shrimp Kebabs 88

Garlic Fries 73

Garlic Herb Crusted Lamb 38

Graham Cracker Cheesecake 99

Green Beans With Sun-dried Tomatoes And Feta 43

Green Curry Beef 33

Grilled Apple Fries With Caramel Cream Cheese Dip 90

Grilled Artichokes With Garlic Aioli 45

Grilled Banana S'mores 94

Grilled Carrots With Honey Glazed 82

Grilled Cornish Hens 65

Grilled Kielbasa And Pineapple Kebabs 16

Grilled Sausage Mix 11

Grilled Strawberry Pound Cake 95

Grilled Vegetable Pizza 55

Grilled Vegetable Quesadillas 53

H

Herb And Pesto Stuffed Pork Loin 28

Herbed Grilled Chicken Thighs 68

Homemade Bbq Chicken Pizza 76

Homemade Teriyaki Pork Ribs 33

Honey Rosemary Chicken 58

Honey-walnut Shrimp 88

I

Italian Sausage And Peppers 30

K

Kidney Beans Oatmeal In Peppers 56

Korean-style Steak Tips 39

L

Lemon And Rosemary Chicken 57

Lemon Dijon Vinaigrette 72

Lemony Blackberry Crisp 97

Lime Chicken With Cilantro 58

Loaded Zucchini Boats 47

M

Mayonnaise-mustard Chicken 61

Mini Turkey Meatloaves With Carrot 64

Mixed Berry And Cream Cheese Puff Pastries 91

Mom's Lemon-pepper Salmon 84

Mozzarella Broccoli Calzones 54

Mozzarella Sticks 73

Mushroom And Squash Toast 22

N

Nut And Seed Muffins 24

Nutty Chicken Tenders 59

O

Oatmeal And Carrot Cookie Cups 96

Olives, Kale, And Pecorino Baked Eggs 20

One-pot Nachos 79

Orange And Anise Cake 97

Orange And Honey Glazed Duck With Apples 70

Orange Cake 92

Orange Coconut Cake 94

P

Peaches-and-cake Skewers 98

Peanut Butter-chocolate Bread Pudding 89

Pecan Pie 101

Pepperoni And Bell Pepper Pockets 28

Perfect Grilled Asparagus 50

Pesto Egg Croissantwiches 14

Pork Sausage With Cauliflower Mash 40

Potato And Prosciutto Salad 25

Potato Cheese Crusted Chicken 66

Potatoes With Zucchinis 44

Pound Cake With Mixed Berries 100

Pumpkin Pudding 102

R

Ranch And Cheddar Pork Chops 36

Rib Eye Steak With Rosemary Butter 31

Roasted Cajun Turkey 60

Roasted Chicken Tenders With Veggies 66

Roasted Mixed Nuts 75

Rosemary Baked Cashews 78

Rosemary Turkey Scotch Eggs 67

Rum Grilled Pineapple Sundaes 92

S

Sausage Ratatouille 35

Shrimp Boil 86

Simple Corn Biscuits 103

Simple Ratatouille 48

Simple Whole Chicken Bake 69

Smoky Paprika Pork And Vegetable Kabobs 27

Spaghetti Squash Lasagna 38

Spiced Turkey Tenderloin 70

Spicy Bbq Chicken Drumsticks 63

Spicy Beef Lettuce Wraps 32

Spicy Chicken Kebabs 62

Spicy Pork Chops With Carrots And Mushrooms 31

Spicy Pork With Candy Onions 30

Spinach Omelet 20

Sriracha Golden Cauliflower 46

Steak And Lettuce Salad 26

Strawberry Pizza 104

Strawberry-glazed Turkey 62

Stuffed Bell Peppers With Italian Maple-glazed Sausage 13

Stuffed Spinach Chicken Breast 63

Stuffed-onion Burgers 39

Summer Squash And Zucchini Salad 52

Supersized Family Pizza Omelet 22

Sweet And Spicy Corn On The Cob 54

Sweet Chili Turkey Kebabs 65

T

Tilapia With Cilantro And Ginger 86

Tofu, Carrot And Cauliflower Rice 51

Tomato-corn Frittata With Avocado Dressing 12

Tomato-stuffed Grilled Sole 87

Tonkatsu 37

Turkey Stuffed Bell Peppers 61

U

Ultimate Coconut Chocolate Cake 99

V

Vanilla Scones 98

Vegetable And Cheese Stuffed Tomatoes 43

Veggie Taco Pie 50

W

Western Omelet 11

Z

Zucchini And Onions Au Gratin 46

Made in the USA
Columbia, SC
24 May 2024

36149276R00061